DATE DUE

Community Leadership

Number Three: Metropolitan Politics Series

COMMUNITY

LEADERSHIP

THE REGIONAL PLAN ASSOCIATION
OF NEW YORK

Forbes B. Hays

COLUMBIA UNIVERSITY PRESS
New York and London 1965

Forbes B. Hays, who received his Ph.D. from Columbia in 1963, is Assistant Professor of Government at Carleton College, Northfield, Minnesota.

Preface

This study is an outgrowth of my conviction, developed when I was associated with a Regional Plan Association study in 1957–58, that RPA is a unique civic experiment. Of all the thousands of voluntary citizens' organizations in the New York metropolitan area, it is the only group that has tried to mobilize a broad regional leadership to attack problems of planning and development on a metropolitan areawide basis. Its founders were insisting on the essential unity of the metropolitan region as far back as the second decade of the twentieth century. Publication of *The Regional Plan of New York and Its Environs* (1929) and the subsequent organization of the RPA have constituted probably the paramount effort to organize metropolitan community leadership around a planning focus. Since the preparation of this manuscript, the RPA has secured funds from several foundations for making a new regional plan, which promises to be one of the most significant ventures yet undertaken in regional research and leadership organization. This study was undertaken in the belief that analysis of such an organization would be a rewarding study in organizational dynamics and would provide some clues to the nature and prospects of the regional leadership that is gradually emerging in large metropolitan areas.

This study would not have been possible without the active cooperation at every juncture of the Regional Plan Association and its staff. In particular, C. McKim Norton, now President of the Association, and John P. Keith, Executive Vice-President, have generously facilitated this study with many kinds of assistance and encouragement. My association with Henry Fagin while he was RPA's Planning Director was a uniquely valuable opportunity to learn something of the breadth and depth of planning concerns from one of the profession's ablest minds. Other members of the RPA staff—especially William B. Shore, Information Director; Richard C. Jorgensen, formerly Membership Secretary; and Sarah Smith, Librarian—were also extremely helpful. Areas Director Ernest Erber furnished important information on the background and development of RPA's New Jersey Committee.

This work was aided by grants from the Metropolitan Region Program of Columbia University. Assistance in typing the original manuscript was provided by Carleton College. A special debt is owed to Wallace S. Sayre, who first brought me into contact with RPA and provided much encouragement throughout, and to David B. Truman. It was under their guidance that this study was conceived.

Finally, I owe a unique obligation to my wife, whose persistent encouragement, criticism, editorial assistance, and secretarial help made completion of this book possible.

FORBES B. HAYS

May, 1964

Contents

Tables

Metropolitan Politics Series

This is the third in the series of books resulting from the metropolitan study program begun at Columbia University in 1957 and supported by a grant from the Ford Foundation.

The faculty committee supervising this program and serving as editors of the series are Wallace S. Sayre, Chairman, Richard E. Neustadt and David B. Truman of the Department of Public Law and Government of Columbia University, and William N. Cassella, Jr., of the National Municipal League.

Community Leadership

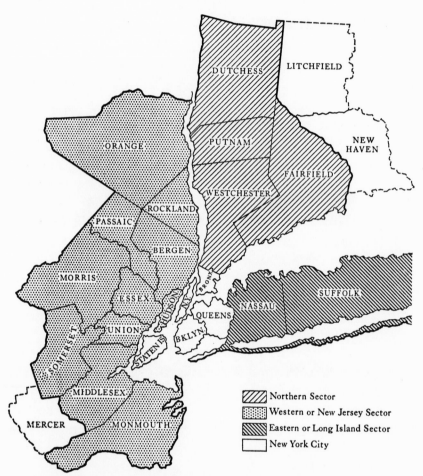

Northern Sector

Western or New Jersey Sector

Eastern or Long Island Sector

New York City

POLITICAL MAP OF THE NEW YORK REGION

SOURCE: *Institute of Public Administration*

Introduction

It has become commonplace to note that the major proportion of Americans today live in metropolitan areas. A growing literature has documented this condition—population movements, dislocations, proliferation of governmental units, "urban sprawl," the battle against the slums, and all the attendant problems of achieving a tolerable degree of amenity and community. With the growing population and geographical spread of metropolitan regions, the range of social, economic, political, and physical characteristics conventionally labeled "urban" and identified with central cities has become inextricably linked with the rest of the metropolis. The social, economic, and political viability of every segment of the region is related to some degree to that of every other part.

If the metropolitan area is in fact a physical and social reality, it must be recognized and treated as such if rational control of the environment is to be attained. Most observers seem to agree that the exercise of market forces and personal choices does not yield a rational or desirable result unless channeled by appropriate broad policy guidelines. Community leadership that can comprehend the relationships that make up a metropolitan region and that can formulate and promote policy alternatives is essential.

The broad concern of this study is metropolitan community leadership. This is an elusive phenomenon. Perhaps, in many regions, there is really no such thing; or perhaps it exists only in a prenatal stage. Nevertheless, there is wide agreement that such leadership should exist, and many are seeking to bring it

into being. This study is the story of one such effort that has
been going on for more than thirty years in the nation's largest
metropolitan area. Because of the much greater size and complexity of the New York metropolitan region as compared with
other regions, the problems of organizing metropolitan areawide leadership are probably more acute than elsewhere. This
study points up, therefore, perhaps in exaggerated form, the
problems and possibilities of organizing civic leadership on a
metropolitan regional basis.

The Regional Plan Association of New York, Inc., is concerned with the coordinated planning of land uses, transportation, and other public facilities in the tri-state twenty-two-
county area centering on the Port of New York.[1] Scarcely any
consciousness of a metropolitan region existed in New York
during the second decade of the twentieth century, when the
idea of a comprehensive regional plan was first formulated by
a small group of distinguished business and civic leaders. Foundation support was secured for a comprehensive survey and
plan for the New York region. The result was *The Regional
Plan of New York and Its Environs,* published in 1929, a landmark in the literature of planning. It was the world's first
metropolitan plan and remains today probably the outstanding
instance of large-scale comprehensive planning for a major
metropolitan area.

This metropolitan plan was the RPA's reason for being. The
Association was formed in 1929 to promote the adoption of the
projects and policies recommended in the Regional Plan and
to encourage the establishment of official planning agencies
throughout the region.

This was a singularly ambitious undertaking. The new organization addressed itself to the planning problems of a region
lying in three states, occupying almost 7,000 square miles, con-
taining (in 1929) well over 9 million inhabitants, and possessing
what has been termed "one of the great unnatural wonders of
the world; that is, a governmental arrangement perhaps more

complicated than any other that mankind has yet contrived or allowed to happen." [2]

This regional focus of interest differentiates RPA from other civic organizations, like the City Club in New York or the Commercial Club in Chicago, that make plans or promote planning. City planning has been the focus of most such groups. However difficult the transition from plan to reality may be, the city planning enthusiasts at least know where the formal authority for carrying out the plan is located. Also, there are other structures of power—political parties, bureaucrats, other interest groups—seeking to influence the same decision-makers. A viable power structure provides scope for bargaining and negotiation. At the regional level, no such structured political environment exists. A regionally-oriented group must cope with a seemingly infinite number of decision points in the array of state, local, and federal agencies whose actions affect regional development, plus the various public authorities (like the Port of New York Authority) in the region. The highly fragmented, pluralistic political pattern of "islands of power" found by Sayre and Kaufman in their study of New York City suggests almost infinite complexity and disorganization at the regional level. [3]

Faced with such an environment, a group like the RPA not only must devise viable policy conceptions based on the best research but, more than most civic organizations, must also give systematic attention to strategies of leadership and implementation. The RPA has been aware of the demanding role it has set for itself. The way in which this leadership role has been interpreted, carried out, and related to other organizational objectives has varied throughout the Association's history. At times the leadership role has almost disappeared, so demanding were its requirements. The primary object of this study is to trace and explain the development of RPA's institutional role as a vehicle of metropolitan community leadership. It is focused on RPA's basic commitments concerning policies, organization, and strategy—how these commitments were formed, how they are mutually related, how they have affected the organization, and how they have changed over time in response to both internal and external developments.

This study does not purport to treat all aspects of RPA's experience. Though the treatment is roughly chronological, it is not designed as a history of the RPA. Many aspects of RPA's operations that would be of considerable interest in other contexts (such as many of RPA's technical and professional achievements) are largely omitted except as they bear on RPA's leadership role. The treatment is largely internal because the assertion of a systematically conceived leadership role has developed very gradually over a considerable period of time. RPA has consciously undertaken a leadership role as a top organizational priority only in very recent years. The development of this role over time is a central concern of this study.

Analysis of internal group processes involves certain research problems that must be recognized, even though they cannot be fully resolved. Data for this study have come from RPA's publications, from the minutes of the meetings of the board of directors and the executive committee, from the files, correspondence, internal memoranda, and records of the Association, to which the writer was generously given unrestricted access, and from numerous interviews with directors, staff members, and others. Interpretation of these kinds of data necessarily requires the researcher to make discriminations and judgments. Written records seldom tell the whole story, interviewer and subject may view the same events in very different frames of reference, and considerable selectivity in off-hand recollections of events long past is surely to be expected. Errors of detail have doubtless crept in. More likely, perhaps, some relevant details may have been omitted, and the judgments and intuition of the writer are certainly not infallible. Nevertheless, with these qualifications, it is believed that available evidence amply substantiates the interpretations advanced here.

CHAPTER I

Origins

Formal organization is not necessarily the point of a group's actual origins. Formal organization, rather, often represents the achievement of a particular frequency of interaction, an achievement that may have been preceded by considerable activity of a less formal, structured nature.[1] An understanding of the circumstances of a group's origin and of the patterns of interaction preceding it helps to account for many of the group's commitments, values, and purposes and for the way these are embodied in the organizational structure. The period of formal organization is one in which a number of crucial, perhaps irreversible, choices are made which permanently affect the organization.[2] An account of the origins of a group helps to clarify the conditions that guided these critical decisions.

The formal organization of the Regional Plan Association in 1929 was the culmination of a series of events dating back nearly to the turn of the century. The immediate background for the establishment of the Association was the completion of *The Regional Plan of New York and Its Environs*. This uniquely ambitious planning venture embodied much of the basic doctrine and program of the Association and occupied an assortment of planners, architects, engineers, and civic leaders for almost a decade. The efforts that culminated in this large undertaking date, in turn, considerably further back.

The late nineteenth and early twentieth centuries were a period of experimentation with a wide variety of reformist measures. Along with the direct primary, "trust-busting," scientific management, municipal research bureaus, good-government crusades, and the like, the city-planning movement aroused considerable interest and enthusiasm in some quarters. Like many of the other movements of the era, it was a more or less "nonpolitical" approach to civic salvation, as well as an aesthetically appealing cause.

Charles Norton and the Burnham Plan of Chicago

One of the leading figures of the planning movement in this era was the architect Daniel Burnham. A visionary apostle of comprehensive planning, Burnham preached:

Make no little plans; they have no magic to stir men's blood and probably themselves will not be realized. Make big plans; aim high in hope and work, remembering that a noble, logical diagram once recorded will never die, but long after we are gone will be a living thing, asserting itself with growing intensity.[3]

Burnham's zeal and sense of mission were contagious; many of those who encountered this planner and his work came away converted to the planning movement.

One such enthusiast of Burnham's comprehensive planning was Charles Dyer Norton, who first conceived the idea of a regional plan for the New York area. Norton, an insurance executive in Chicago during most of the first decade of the century, had been president of the Commercial Club of Chicago in 1906, when that organization engaged Burnham to make a master plan for Chicago. (Frederic Delano, another figure prominent in the New York Regional Plan movement, was also an officer of the Commercial Club at this time.)[4]

Burnham's Chicago Plan is regarded as a landmark of the planning movement. Published by the Commercial Club in 1909, Burnham's plan was greeted with considerable interest and publicity in professional and civic leadership circles throughout the country. The famed architect Charles McKim wrote Burnham that the Chicago Plan "stands as one of your

monuments—greater far than all of them put together, in fact." [5]
Burnham's enraptured biographer, Charles Moore, states that
the Chicago Plan "embodies the principles underlying all city-
planning, past, present, and future; and it glows with the enthusiasm with which the real creator inspires his work." [6]

The Commercial Club presented Burnham's plan to the city
of Chicago, with a recommendation that a city planning commission be appointed to continue planning for the city's development. Such a commission was officially created, and prominent civic leaders, including many who had been associated
with the Commercial Club, were appointed to it. Many of the
plan's proposals were carried out over the next several years.

Such was the experience that Norton carried with him when
he left Chicago in 1909. A convert to Burnham's philosophy,
Norton stated that in starting the Chicago Plan project, "We
finally got into our stride only when we decided to quit nib-
bling at Court House site problems and do something big
enough to include all of Chicago and its environs." [7] Norton
left Chicago to go to Washington to become Assistant Secretary
of the Treasury, a post he held for about a year. He then became Secretary to the President in 1910. William Howard Taft
credited Norton with suggesting and making possible the Taft
Efficiency and Economy Commission, one of the pioneering
efforts in studying governmental organization, and with advo-
cacy of an executive budget.[8]

Early Planning Efforts in New York

It was from this background of experience in city planning
and in administrative reform that Norton came to New York
in 1911 as vice-president of the First National Bank of New
York. Immediately he became interested in promoting planning in New York. He later wrote his colleague in the Chicago
Plan venture, Frederic Delano: "When I first came to New

York in 1911, our efforts for the Chicago Plan were still fresh in mind. The thought kept recurring that New York should have a plan and should take a vital interest in it." [9]

Norton soon found an ally in George McAneny, Manhattan Borough President. McAneny, like Norton, was a reform-minded leader who had a long and distinguished career in journalism, law, politics, and planning. From 1892 until 1903 McAneny was an officer of both the National Civil Service Reform League and the New York City Civil Service Reform Association, and was co-author, in 1899, of New York State's Civil Service law. Before becoming Borough President in 1910, he served four years as president of the City Club of New York, an organization similar to the Commercial Club in Chicago. The City Club organized a Committee on the City Plan under McAneny's leadership. The major concern of this committee was the "lack of any curbs on the high buildings down in the lower part of town," [10] according to McAneny. Their activities resulted, after McAneny was elected to the Board of Estimate, in the appointment of a Zoning Commission and a Transit Commission by the Board, each with an annual appropriation from the city of $25,000.[11] McAneny, who sponsored both of these commissions, served as chairman of the Transit Commission.

McAneny responded to Norton's interest in city planning with the appointment of a third commission, this one on city planning. In 1914 McAneny became President of the Board of Aldermen and persuaded the Board to create an official Committee on the City Plan, consisting of the borough presidents. What this *ex officio* committee was to do was not clear. As a civic counterpart to this body, McAneny appointed an advisory committee on the city plan, consisting of twenty-four business and professional figures, with Norton as chairman.

Norton wrote to Delano that "McAneny has a splendid zeal for City Planning," although "I think his interest is more in transit and zoning and limiting heights of buildings than in the sweeping Dan Burnham notions that you and I were imbued with." [12] Of the work of the advisory body that he chaired, Norton wrote: "Our advisory committee met solemnly in a beautiful room in the City Hall once or twice and wisely resolved to give our advice only when asked for, which was never." [13] The borough presidents failed to function as a planning group.

The major result of McAneny's operations in the planning field in this period was the adoption of New York City's first comprehensive zoning ordinance in 1916. This was an extremely important development, and its accomplishment probably dulled the enthusiasm of political and civic leaders for more comprehensive plans. Although Norton recognized the significance of the zoning ordinance, he was convinced that broader and more far-reaching efforts were needed.

Persuaded that the committee of the borough presidents was only a paper organization, Norton attempted to establish a large-scale planning project without relying on city officials. Late in 1915, he called a meeting of his advisory committee, and suggested organizing a private citizens' group to finance and develop a comprehensive regional plan. In this way New York might duplicate the planning achievements of Chicago.

A most important departure in Norton's proposal was his insistence that the entire metropolitan region be included in a single plan. Since he was proposing a private organization outside governmental auspices, there was no need to confine the plan to the single political jurisdiction of New York City. Norton suggested that planning in New York had not gotten off the ground because "no plan has ever been projected here on a scale vast enough to capture the interest and the imagination of this group of cities, towns and villages which is New York." [14] How vast a scale did Norton have in mind?

From the City Hall a circle must be swung which will include the Atlantic Highlands and Princeton; the lovely Jersey hills back of Morristown and Tuxedo; the incomparable Hudson as far as Newburgh; the Westchester lakes and ridges, to Bridgeport and beyond, and all of Long Island.[15]

He estimated that such a plan would take about five years to complete and would cost about $200,000.[16] He proposed to raise this sum by voluntary contributions.

Norton's suggestion came to naught; he wrote to Delano that "the usual timid notions prevailed." [17] A member of the advisory committee wrote to Norton, voicing the typical reaction:

It does not seem to me wise to include so wide an area in your City plan, especially as so much of the territory is entirely beyond New York jurisdiction. I do not myself see the connection between Princeton, Tuxedo, and Stamford, and our immediate problems, and I think that the issue will be greatly confused if so much is attempted. I think also that such a group as you suggest representing all this territory would be a hopeless, unwieldly body. . . . In any plan we may make, I think we should remember the danger of over-planning; that is, going too far beyond public opinion.[18]

The greatest difficulty was finance. Norton's business commitments did not allow him time to organize a fund-raising operation, and no ready source of funds seemed available. There was some discussion of asking John D. Rockefeller, Jr., for backing, but this suggestion was not acted upon. Norton's regional planning project thus aroused no particular enthusiasm and met with insuperable financial difficulties.

Other events also dampened Norton's hopes. His good friend McAneny resigned the Borough Presidency in 1916; in 1918 John F. Hylan became Mayor, and "everything that George McAneny had built up in the City Hall was swept into limbo." [19] According to McAneny:

The Mayor, . . . Mr. Hylan, was very much against all of these new things. He didn't believe in them. He announced at one of the hearings down there that he didn't believe in the freaks of these "art artists," and so on. I had previously gotten $25,000 a year from the city to run the other commissions [transit and zoning], and it was repeated with this one. Hylan commissioned to have it cut off so that there was nothing left.[20]

These developments confirmed Norton in his growing skepticism of accomplishing a bold planning effort under official auspices. Neither public nor private sponsorship of planning seemed possible at this point.

The Russell Sage Foundation

Norton's dream of a regional plan for New York might have been laid to rest had he not become a trustee and the treasurer of the Russell Sage Foundation in 1918. The Russell Sage Foundation is a philanthropic organization committed by the terms of its bequest to spend at least 25 percent of its revenues for the benefit of the New York area.[21] Early in 1919, in a discussion of possible future programs for the Foundation, Norton renewed his proposal for a regional plan.

The Foundation's president, Robert de Forest, found the scheme too grandiose and asked Norton to scale it down to more manageable proportions, "something more specific and local like playgrounds or rural parks." [22] Other objections centered around the expense of the project and its effects on other Russell Sage programs. Norton now estimated the cost of a regional plan to be $300,000. He was asked to draw up a memorandum demonstrating the economic and social relationships of the vast area he wished to include.

Norton did not make any attempt to reduce the scope of his proposal; he pointed instead to the Chicago Plan as evidence of the efficacy of large-scale planning. Unconvinced, the other officers of the Foundation still regarded the project as too global.

Finally, in December, 1920, the regional planning proposal was revived by Alfred White, a Russell Sage trustee strongly interested in expanding and broadening the Foundation's program. This time the trustees were more receptive. On February 7, 1921, a committee consisting of Norton, de Forest, and John M. Glenn, general director of the Foundation, was appointed and authorized to spend up to $25,000 for a preliminary investigation of the proposal. The committee engaged Nelson P.

Lewis, a former city engineer, who had been chief consultant
to McAneny's committee on the city plan, to conduct the necessary studies.

Three months later, a much more substantial commitment
to the project was made: an additional $25,000 was appropri-
ated for the committee's immediate use, and the committee was
authorized to spend up to $300,000 over the next several years.[23]
The committee was enlarged to include two more trustees:
Dwight Morrow, a partner of J. P. Morgan and Company, and
Frederic Delano, head of several railroad lines and vice-gover-
nor of the Federal Reserve Board.

Public announcement of the project was delayed until fifteen
months of preliminary staff work had been completed. When
the venture was announced in May, 1922, some of the area's
most prestigious civic figures spoke on its behalf. These included Elihu Root, Herbert Hoover, John C. Carty, Charles
Dana Gibson, Lillian Wald, and Mrs. August Belmont.[24] Four
months later an additional grant of $500,000 was made to the
committee. What the historians of the Russell Sage Foundation
termed "the most ambitious single enterprise sponsored by the
Foundation" [25] was now to begin.

What was to become *The Regional Plan of New York and Its
Environs* had begun as no more than a gleam in Charles Norton's eye. Like many important civic enterprises, the Regional
Plan would probably never have existed without the active support of a philanthropic foundation. Norton's was an advanced
conception; such an idea was not likely to find support outside
a group willing to take certain risks and indulge some experi-
mental notions. Even so, it took considerable prodding by one
of its own members for the Russell Sage board to see the merits
of so broad a plan.

The Regional Plan was not launched on any great tide of
public sentiment; the Foundation was acting here as a substitute for governmental and civic support. Such a beginning may

create serious organizational and leadership problems later. If a going enterprise is to be maintained after foundation support is exhausted, a potent leadership and constituency must be recruited. The obstacles Norton encountered earlier would eventually have to be faced again.

The Committee on the Regional Plan

Once financial support for a regional plan had been secured, a number of critical decisions had to be made concerning the organization, staff, and scope of the plan and provisions for carrying it out.

The project was designed to bring the best available technical expertise to bear on the problems of the region's physical development without too specific consideration of strategies of implementation. Norton's correspondence records a conversation with Elihu Root in this connection:

I spent two hours with Elihu Root at his apartment and outlined the project to him. He was intensely interested and encouraged me heartily. His first thought was that we should make a careful study of the Boroughs and enlist the interest of the key men and women of local political influence; but he finally assented heartily to my proposition that in its early stage we could wisely ignore all personal questions and political considerations; that we could better concentrate our energies in organizing the ablest possible inquiries as a basis for the largest and finest plans.[26]

Norton reported that the members of the Committee on the Regional Plan were in basic agreement that

We must approach our problem very much as Senator Aldrich approached the problems of monetary reform; that we must organize a series of well-defined fundamental inquiries, deliberately undertaken, staffed by the ablest men, their results carefully edited for brevity and clarity, and published in attractive form.[27]

Thus, it was decided that the organization of support for the implementation of the plan was not to be built into the planning process itself. In view of his experience in trying to organ-

ize planning projects earlier, Norton was probably convinced
that recruitment of support would be easier when a plan was
already in being. Much of the doctrine of the planning movement also stressed that a plan, if good enough, would make its
own way.

The goal of the project was a forty-year plan which would
embody the best collective judgments and efforts of the ablest
planners, architects, and engineers that could be recruited. Nelson Lewis, who had directed the preliminary staff surveys, died
in 1924 and was succeeded by Thomas Adams, who became
general director of plans and surveys. Adams, a prominent Eng-
lish planner, was a founder of the Garden City Association and
the first president of the Town Planning Institute of Great
Britain and had taught for a time at the Massachusetts Institute
of Technology. A variety of planning experts were brought in
for various aspects of the projects, and several consulting committees of architects and engineers were formed.

Soon after the survey was underway, the Russell Sage trustees
decided to convert the Committee to an autonomous status,
independent of formal ties with or direct control by the Russell
Sage Foundation. There may have been two motives, not unre-
lated, in setting up this arrangement. First, it was believed that
the project would generate more public support if it were an
independent program sponsored by a group of leading community figures.[28] Secondly, the scale of the venture was such
that the Foundation was promoting a project larger than it
could conduct alone without changing the scope of its operations in a fundamental way. The Foundation wanted to maintain its future freedom of action and program and not to narrow its operations solely to planning.

There is no record of a suggestion at this time of a permanent
independent group such as the Regional Plan Association. It is
possible, however, that an additional reason for making the
Committee independent was to facilitate creation of such an

organization later on. The Foundation may have viewed its role as provision of the stimulus for what would become an independent and permanent community enterprise.

Although the Committee was made formally independent of the Russell Sage Foundation, a majority of the Committee was, at all times, constituted by Russell Sage trustees. The Committee's work was financed entirely by the Russell Sage Foundation, and the Committee and its staff were housed in Foundation offices, making considerable use of Foundation staff. The Foundation's total investment in the regional survey and plan, exclusive of office space and unbudgeted staff services, was $1,186,768.[29]

At the same time that the Committee on the Regional Plan was made independent, it was expanded to include six more members. These included the following:

John H. Finley, an associate editor (later editor) of the New York *Times,* had been president of Knox College and City College of New York, New York State Commissioner of Education and president of the State University of New York, editor of *Harper's Weekly,* and a professor of politics at Princeton and was active in philanthropic enterprises, serving as president of the New York Association for the Blind, the National City Welfare Association, the National Recreation Association, and the New York Adult Education Council and as secretary of the State Charities Aid Association.

Henry James, a lawyer and writer, was active in philanthropy, including service as manager and trustee of the Rockefeller Institute for Medical Research, and was a trustee of the Carnegie Corporation.

George McAneny, then serving as executive manager of the New York *Times,* had just been named chairman of the New York State Transit Commission.

Frank L. Polk, a lawyer who had served on the New York Civil Service Commission and the New York City Board of

Education, had been New York City Corporation Counsel and
Under Secretary of State and Acting Secretary of State in Wood-
row Wilson's administration and was a director of six banking,
railroad, and insurance firms.

Frederick B. Pratt, a partner of Charles Pratt and Company,
was president of a building firm and of the Pratt Institute.

Lawson Purdy, a lawyer, had been president of the New York
City Department of Taxes and Assessments for eleven years,
was active in the Charity Organization Society, National Information Bureau, and St. Andrew's Convalescent Hospital, and
was later to succeed to the presidency of the Russell Sage
Foundation.[30]

This enlarged Committee was designed to provide the most
prestigious possible sponsorship for the regional plan. The
Committee was chaired by Charles Norton until his death in
1923, when his old friend and planning colleague Frederic Delano succeeded him. Norton's place was not filled after his
death, making the group a ten-man committee. It was reduced
to nine in 1927, when Dwight Morrow accepted appointment
as U.S. Ambassador to Mexico. This prestige and the Russell
Sage Foundation's ample financial backing assured that the resulting plan would be received with due respect and attention
by the community.

In addition to the technical staff working under the Committee's general supervision, the Committee recruited a public
relations staff which was busily engaged during the making of
the regional survey and plan. The Committee did not seek
widespread mass support; Delano, in an early memorandum on
public relations, wrote

A new Division has been suggested for Public Relations, because
I believe this phase of the subject needs attention, but I am not
particularly impressed with the need of newspaper publicity. When
we have something to say, we will get publicity enough. However,
we do not want unfavorable criticism, nor do we want that inertia
which is more deadly than opposition. It seems to me we must have
a live, personal contact with the organizations within the 50-mile

radius, which are interested and willing to work on the subject of a better plan for New York and its Environs. We must be the clearing house for the city planning effort of 400 cities, towns and villages.[31]

The public relations effort was directed by Flavel Shurtleff, a planner, secretary of the National Conference on City Planning since 1909, and author of *Carrying Out the City Plan*.

According to much accepted planning doctrine, the primary requirement for carrying out plans was the creation of an official planning body in every jurisdiction. At this stage, there appears to have been somewhat less concern than in the future with the powers these boards should possess. The crucial factor then was simply to get the planning function officially recognized, preferably by the creation of an "independent" or "non-political" commission of citizens not responsible to the political executive.[32]

Delano's mandate on public relations was interpreted in terms of this standard doctrine. The public relations effort was largely devoted to propagation of the planning gospel and helping to establish official planning agencies in the region's political jurisdictions. The number of official planning boards in the region grew from 10 in 1923 to 87 by 1931, when the last volume of the Regional Plan was published.[33] Much of this proliferation of planning was a result of the efforts of the Committee's public relations staff. Thus, to the staff, Delano's eschewing of "newspaper publicity" and his emphasis on "live personal contact" meant the promotion of planning, reliance on expertise, and perhaps skepticism of anything suggesting "political pressure" tactics.

There is, perhaps, some ambiguity in Delano's statement. It could also be read as reliance on a regional "elite" composed of top-drawer community figures, who would be activated through personal contacts and who would quietly counsel with public officials, advising and persuading them.

These interpretations are not mutually exclusive; both figure prominently in the RPA's later definitions of its organizational role.

The Regional Plan

The end result of the investigation that began in 1922 was the publication of twelve volumes. Ten "survey volumes" appeared from 1928 to 1931, each describing and analyzing some aspect of the region's physical development.[34] In 1929 and 1931 the two "Plan volumes" appeared. These were the end product to which the survey volumes had been preliminary. The first of these, published in 1929 (*The Graphic Regional Plan*), contained maps illustrating the proposed plan and a detailed description of the 470 physical projects that constituted the Plan. The second volume, *The Building of the City* (1931), presented and illustrated the planning principles on which the Regional Plan was based.

The Regional Plan was regarded as an advancement beyond the "city beautiful" emphasis that had characterized earlier planning efforts, such as Burnham's Chicago Plan. The Committee reported concerning its efforts that

The work . . . has differed from much city planning in that the effort has not been primarily for beauty, although the whole plan tends to that end, but always the social factor has been emphasized. The aim has been not only to build noble structures, highways, and parks "to endure," but to preserve civilization, and no element entering into this consideration has been overlooked.[35]

The Plan rested on the premise that "the manner in which land is used and in which the functions and bulks of buildings upon the land are distributed and related, lies at the root of all urban problems."[36] Considerable point is made of the relationships between land use and transportation patterns, and the Plan reflects the growing concern of the planning movement with problems of central-city congestion and adequate transportation facilities. A present-day authority describes the concern of planners of this period:

Then came, early in this century, a development of congested down-
town construction. Probably if there was one technological feature
that was most responsible, it was the evolution of structural steel
for building. But transportation technology in the form of rapid
transit facilities also had its bearing on intensive (and mixed up)
growth in the middles of cities. . . . Then came the automobile,
adding a new kind of congestion to what was already present in
the central areas. During the 1920's, perhaps the most important
single concern of city planning was traffic congestion, traffic improvement, and thoroughfare plans.[37]

When the Regional Plan was being made, New York was not
ready to cope with the automobile age. There were, at that
time, no fixed crossings of the Hudson River (the Holland
Tunnel was being constructed) and only three crossings of the
East River (there are now eight), nor were there express highways anywhere in the metropolitan area. The Regional Plan,
consequently, presented a series of detailed proposals dealing
with the development and coordination of rail, automobile, and
air transportation. The proposals included

new railway belt lines, connections with old lines and new water-
front lines and new union passenger terminals; a series of proposals
with regard to the development of a suburban rapid transit system;
new railroad crossings of major waterways; waterway projects and
development of water areas; regional highways, including a metropolitan loop, inner routes, radial routes, outer circumferential
routes, a metropolitan bypass, express highways and supplementary
routes; minor regional highways, parkways, and boulevards; . . .
airports and landing facilities.[38]

The planners realized that new transportation facilities alone
might result in increased congestion. Hence, stronger zoning
controls and limitations on the bulk of building were advocated. Paul Windels, a past president of the Association, explained the basis of these features of the Plan:

The street system, with a capacity designed to serve a city with an
over-all average height of six stories, could by the uncontrolled
exploitation of land, have superimposed over it not one but several
or more new layers of cities with no corresponding increase in the
underlying street capacity. The result could be traffic chaos.[39]

The Plan preferred lateral to vertical expansion and called for leaving open space on all sides of a skyscraper. The relation of building density to street capacity was thus emphasized.

The Plan went beyond recommending controls on future construction in the central city. It called for "recentralization" to relieve central-city congestion:

not spreading industry evenly over the map but creating new centers for it here and there. Similarly, instead of completely decentralizing residence areas, and imposing on commuters the ever increasing "frictions of space," they would diffuse it into "compact residential neighborhoods" throughout the whole urban region, integrated with industrial sections so as to reduce distances between homes and places of work.[40]

The Plan envisioned an outward movement of population in clusters centering around major transportation arteries (hence the crucial role of transportation planning). With proper standards of zoning and subdivision control in the suburban areas, the estimated 1965 population of 21 million people could be accommodated so that

Every family could, if it wanted, as far as space is concerned, have a house of its own on a lot 40 by 100 feet with ample sunlight, and even so, only one-fourth of the land in the region would be occupied for residential purposes.[41]

The other major object of the Plan was "to bring people in closer touch with open spaces." Prior to the Regional Plan, there were no major plans in being for parks, recreation, or other open-space needs. The Plan contained detailed recommendations for public parks throughout the region. Accessibility of open spaces was seen as an important factor in planning residential developments and in designing an adequate transportation system.

The Regional Plan was thus an integrated conception, attempting to relate systematically several major factors of regional development, starting from a statement of the problem and a set of priorities that were a compound of what the survey research revealed and what the planners' judgment and intuition suggested.

The Regional Plan Association

Immediately before the publication of the first volume of the Plan, the Regional Plan Association was formed and incorporated. It has not been possible to determine precisely who at what time first suggested a continuing civic organization. It is clear, however, that the idea originated within the Committee on the Regional Plan. According to a member of the Committee, John Glenn, "The Committee and its friends realized that the Plan would not go into effect automatically after its publication." [42] The groundwork for the RPA was laid at a dinner meeting of a small group of prominent civic figures organized by Lawson Purdy, a member of the Committee, in December, 1928. This group included but was not limited to members of the Committee. There was a general awareness that the Regional Plan had not been a response to an upsurge of public interest in planning, and there was general agreement that some organizational structure should be established to keep the Plan alive and in the public eye until it was carried out.

Over the next few weeks several drafts of a constitution for the new Association were prepared. Purdy, with the assistance of a few members of the Russell Sage staff, was chiefly responsible for this task. It was agreed from the outset that the Association should be governed by a self-perpetuating board of directors. The officers of the Association were to be nominated by the directors and elected at the Association's annual meeting, to which the Association's individual members would be invited. The organization would be effectively governed by its directors, with nominal membership participation at the annual meeting, in much the same fashion that a business corporation is governed. Thus, though membership was open to anyone at a nominal annual subscription, there was no particular

effort to implement a significant degree of membership participation and control. This was not surprising, as the Committee
on the Regional Plan had been a very small elite group that
had not sought a mass following.

The size of the board was a problem for the drafters of the
constitution. Purdy at first reportedly leaned toward a board
little or no larger than the nine-member Committee on the
Regional Plan. Members of the Committee's staff, more interested in board participation, favored a larger group. A board
of twenty-one members was agreed upon.[43]

A further problem to be resolved was the term of office of
directors. In one of Purdy's early drafts seven-year terms were
provided for; those of the original directors would be staggered,
with the terms of three directors ending each year. Staff members favored a system of three-year terms, with the terms of
seven directors expiring each year. The rationale of the staff's
point of view was explained in a memorandum to Purdy:

in order to make possible a greater regional representation and a
greater feeling on the part of the membership of participation in
the selection of the governing body. I do not fear that this will
result in any upheaval or unseating of the Directors originally
selected . . . ; whereas electing only three Directors, in my opinion,
would make it very much like a closed corporation, and I am convinced that the psychology of broad participation is a sound one.[44]

Purdy came around to this view, believing that the board
should avoid the appearance of being a narrow and tightly knit
group, and the final draft of the constitution incorporated the
three-year terms. Purdy approved this draft two days before
the first official meeting of the new Association.

The first meeting was held on April 4, 1929, with Purdy
presiding. The constitution was formally adopted, and the directors that Purdy had recruited were duly elected. All the
members of the Committee on the Regional Plan except Frederic Delano became directors; five more were chosen from the
Russell Sage Foundation staff or the Committee staff—Shelby

Harrison, Wayne Heydecker, Frederick Keppel, Lawrence Orton, and Flavel Shurtleff. (Two of these, Heydecker and Shurtleff, resigned within a few months to take staff positions in RPA. Orton did likewise in 1931.) The other eight members were recruited from outside the Committee and Foundation orbit through personal contacts by members of the Committee, primarily Purdy. Almost two-thirds of the board was constituted by persons directly involved in the making of the Re· gional Plan.

As a means of establishing a broader base of support, the Committee hoped to attract some distinguished community figure who had not been connected with the Committee or with the Russell Sage Foundation to serve as president of the Association. The presidency was offered to E. H. Outerbridge, a prominent merchant. Outerbridge agreed to serve on the board but declined the presidency on account of his advancing years and failing health. After Outerbridge declined, the presidency was tendered to George McAneny, a member of the Regional Plan Committee and long-time leader in public affairs. McAneny accepted and served until 1940.

The Association was launched financially by a grant of $25,000 from the Russell Sage Foundation. The Foundation regarded this as "seed money." It was hoped that the Association would become self-supporting through regular private contributions. Launched on the eve of the depression, RPA was not able to find sufficient independent financial support and was kept alive by a series of Russell Sage grants that, by the mid-1940s, totaled $600,000.[45]

The Committee on the Regional Plan continued its formally separate existence until 1931, when the second Plan volume was published, even though its membership almost completely overlapped with the RPA board. Its files, studies, and what was left of a separate staff were turned over to RPA in 1931, making the amalgamation complete.

The Regional Plan Association thus came into being as a

continuation of the Committee on the Regional Plan. As such, it did not have complete freedom of choice concerning organizational commitments and roles. It inherited the experience, background, and leadership of the Committee. Many of RPA's basic choices and commitments are rooted in this inherited experience. Consequently, this background is essential in understanding the origin and nature of some of RPA's basic commitments. It is to an analysis of those commitments—what they were, their origins, their embodiment in the organization, and their consequences for the organization—to which attention is now directed.

CHAPTER II

Commitments

The distinctive character of an organization is defined by its basic commitments to certain goals, values, and ways of behaving—commitments that cannot be routinely altered but change only with some degree of internal crisis or significant environmental change.[1] The task of this chapter is to examine the set of commitments that came to constitute the organizational character of the Regional Plan Association and to see how these commitments were incorporated into RPA's structure and program.

The commitments discussed here were formed in RPA's early years. They do not necessarily provide a valid description of every facet of RPA's role at all times, but neither are they relevant only to RPA's early history. These commitments have had fundamental significance for RPA at all times and help to indicate how and why RPA has become what it is and to appraise the potentialities and constraints shaping RPA's future.

Doctrinal Commitments

An obvious starting point in the search for organizational goals is the statement of purpose given in the group's constitution. The opening statement in RPA's constitution is of interest for what it omits as well as for what it includes.

Although the circumstances of RPA's origin suggest that a chief purpose was to be promotion of the recommendations of the Regional Plan, this is curiously omitted from the constitution adopted by the Association in 1929. That document states:

The object of the Regional Plan Association, Inc., shall be to foster
county, city, town, and village planning within the region centering on the Port of New York.[2]

It was not until 1934 that this article was amended to include
specific reference to the Regional Plan. The amended article
read:

The object of the Regional Plan Association, Inc., shall be to work
for the realization of the Regional Plan of New York and Its
Environs, subject to such modification as may prove desirable from
time to time, and to foster county, city, town, and village planning
within the region centering on the Port of New York.[3]

The reasons for this omission from the 1929 constitution
are not clear. The framers may have been so imbued with
planning ideology that they felt that adoption of the Regional
Plan would inevitably and automatically follow the creation
of competent planning agencies. Given the intimate link between the Committee on the Regional Plan and the RPA,
however, it is difficult to accept this reasoning as a sufficient
explanation for the omission. Also, given the care and deliberation with which the constitution was drafted, it is hardly likely
that this omission was casual or accidental.

There are at least two other explanations for this omission
which are neither mutually exclusive nor inconsistent with
available evidence. Once the Regional Plan was largely
adopted, recurrent questions arose concerning RPA's role and
even its justification for continued existence. Possibly in antici-
pation of such questions, the framers of the RPA constitution
wished to avoid too explicit a commitment to the Regional
Plan per se, since such a commitment could give the appearance of a definitely limited program, hinting even that RPA
might disband on its completion. They may have wished to
state an organizational purpose that would imply the permanence of the group.

The other reason for this omission might be connected with
the fervent professions, from the early days of the Plan to the

present, of the "nonpolitical" nature of the organization. Commitment to a series of projects, most of which could be executed only by appropriate governmental agencies, might have suggested a "political pressure" orientation which the founders wished to avoid.

There is, of course, no necessary conflict between the goals of promoting the Regional Plan and promoting official planning. The Association did both, although in its early years a preponderance of staff time was spent helping to set up planning agencies. RPA's initial stated goal thus was the promotion of planning, which was presumably to encompass in some sense promotion of the Regional Plan proposals.

THE COMMITMENT TO REGIONALISM

A primary commitment of RPA was its regional focus of interest, transcending the boundaries of existing political jurisdictions. This was the heart of Norton's original idea and was embodied in the Regional Survey and Plan when the region was defined to cover twenty-two counties in three states.

Historically, this may be the most important of RPA's commitments, making it a particularly appropriate vehicle for the organization of regional leadership. This advanced conception has occasionally caused some observers to view RPA as being too nebulous and idealistic in its interests. If, however, the regional focus provoked accusations of vacuity, it also helped to justify both the private sponsorship of the Plan and the existence of RPA. The Regional Plan states:

The fact that the Region lies in three states, and that there are hundreds of public authorities, as well as numerous public utility and trunk railroad corporations who operate within its borders, indicate that the making of a complete regional plan was a task that could not be undertaken by any official group, either existing or likely to be created. It was essential for the plan to be made by an unofficial advisory committee.[4]

This regional focus is also a potential leadership resource

for RPA. Until the Metropolitan Regional Council was formed in 1956, RPA was the sole spokesman for a general regional viewpoint. It was the only group consciously trying to develop a regionwide civic leadership. At times this meant no more than seeking a rough balance of geographical representation on the RPA board; but as RPA's concerns become more salient to larger numbers, its regional focus provides a certain symbolic and moral authority to speak on behalf of broader, more general interests.

COMPREHENSIVE PLANNING

Another of RPA's initial commitments closely related to its regional focus was its commitment to *comprehensive* planning. The idea that successful planning must take account of numerous related factors, none of which should be planned without reference to the others, was a vital part of the planning ideology that Norton had inherited from Burnham. This comprehensiveness is cited as one of the virtues of the Regional Plan. According to Thomas Adams,

The failure of plans to achieve adequate results in the past has been due largely to lack of comprehensive treatment of the combined problems of circulation, utilization of land and building development, for an area large enough to enable problems of urban growth to be understood in proper perspective and in their full significance and relations.[5]

These commitments to comprehensive planning on a regionwide basis were regarded as key factors setting RPA apart from other organizations and agencies. No other group had this particular set of concerns. RPA has often manifested considerable self-consciousness with respect to these commitments, sometimes being characterized as "aloof" by outside observers. It has generally guarded its virtue by keeping other organizations at arm's length, avoiding being drawn into the orbit of the Port Authority, the Citizens Union, or any other body. Its rationale for this has usually been that it operates from a broader

perspective than other groups and should remain free to criticize others from its loftier position.

These policies have often helped to keep RPA "above the
battle" in political conflicts which involved many other civic
groups. RPA has usually managed to limit sharply its involvement to the specifically regional features of public issues. As
a result, RPA has few of either the scars or the successes of
controversial political involvement.

This cautious policy was probably a considerable help to
RPA in maintaining its organizational identity during years
when that identity did not have a firm and substantial social
base. An organization built on tenuous advanced commitments
can readily lose its identity if it becomes indiscriminately involved in political issues. It can also lose contact with reality
if it turns inward for too long.

PHYSICAL PLANNING

The "comprehensiveness" that the Regional Plan stressed
was confined to the physical factors of transportation, land use,
and bulk of buildings and tended to minimize social and political considerations related to these. Lewis Mumford, who
scathingly denounced the Plan, termed it "a sociological failure." [6] The makers of the Regional Plan had anticipated this
criticism:

The belief that planning in the past has been carried out with too
narrow a conception of what needs to be planned has driven many
to the assumption that there can be no limit to the civic problems
that should be dealt with in a plan. If, however, a plan were to
deal with all the physical, economic, and social features of the
city, it would be nothing less than a charter of civilization.[7]

They further stress that the Plan had been based on a large-
scale regional survey, which had investigated economic and
industrial conditions and legal, social, and housing matters as
well as physical problems. Yet the physical emphasis stands out.

It is indisputable that no plan can include every relevant

facet of urban life; but this delimitation, along with some of
the accompanying statements about the efficacy of planning,
suggests a tendency to reduce social, political, and economic
issues to largely physical dimensions. As will be seen, some of
RPA's leaders in later years were severely critical of too narrow
a physical emphasis in these early days.

COORDINATIVE CONSEQUENCES OF A GOOD PLAN

The makers of the Regional Plan had great faith in what
a good plan could accomplish by its own inherent force. They
did not regard the political and administrative fragmentation
of the region as too serious an obstacle. If each jurisdiction
has a competent planning body, their efforts can be coordinated
by the rationality of a well-designed regional plan:

> If the City of New York appoints a planning commission of the
> same quality as was done in Chicago, and other cities and villages
> do likewise; if also persistence is shown in keeping the Regional
> Plan before the public for a long enough term of years to give an
> adequate comprehension of the real character of the civic problems
> and the best means by which these problems can be solved, much
> greater achievements than those listed above [in Chicago] will be
> possible in New York in coming years.[8]

Tampering with governmental structure is not advocated;
indeed, a good plan removes many of the reasons for seeking
structural changes:

> As planning of towns lessens the necessity of incorporating new
> village areas, so, on the other hand, cooperative planning between
> adjacent cities and towns lessens the necessity for extension of the
> city boundaries by inclusion of adjacent areas of towns or villages.
> . . . Many schemes for extension of cities have their chief justifica-
> tion in conditions that could not exist if there were cooperative
> city and town planning. Such schemes are usually resisted by the
> outside communities, and, even when made possible by their con-
> sent, impose heavy burdens of cost on the city that make the con-
> solidation of questionable value.[9]

Although this may have been designed to allay fears of
"metropolitan supergovernment," it seems from the total con-

text of the Plan and related documents to be a fairly accurate statement of the convictions of the founders of RPA. The Association has never officially deviated from this policy of coordination through planning rather than through changes of governmental structure.

The governmental structure of the region provided an additional reason for emphasizing the self-executing properties of a good plan. In 1929 more than 400 municipalities existed in the twenty-two counties. The region lay in three states, with three sets of policies on taxation, state aid to municipalities, and other relevant matters. Only the Port of New York Authority, created in 1921, exercised jurisdiction transcending local boundaries, and its functions were limited and its jurisdiction less than regionwide. In 1929, it was only beginning to shape what has come to be its dominant role and point of view. There was little awareness that the region might be thought of as a meaningful unity for some purposes. Whatever the built-in biases of the planning ideology, the governmental structure of the New York region left the planners with no real alternative to the self-executing-plan doctrine.

Strategies of Action and Influence

RPA's strategies for influencing the course of events in the region were not spelled out in the Regional Plan or in other early expressions of doctrine. At the outset, the leaders of the Committee on the Regional Plan had decided to "ignore all personal questions and political situations" and concentrate on making "the largest and finest plans." The organization of support for the Plan and attendant questions of leadership strategy were postponed and subordinated to the immediate task of plan-making. Having made the Regional Plan, RPA had to determine what its role in promoting its Plan would be.

There was no systematic consideration of this question and no clear-cut organizational commitment in RPA's early years.

Expressions of opinion on this subject were, taken together, ambiguous. Several alternative choices were suggested by RPA's inherited commitments and doctrines.

At one extreme, RPA could take literally the self-executing-plan philosophy. This would confine RPA to a minimal leadership role and might even draw RPA's existence into question. Research and study would be RPA's main function.

There was at least some basis for this view that a good plan is a sufficient leadership force in the Regional Plan. The director of the Committee's staff stated among his basic principles of planning:

We must not overemphasize the value of the administrative processes by which plans are carried out as compared with the technical processes by which plans are made.[10]

The Regional Plan states that

If a city plan presents a sound conception of order and beauty in building, and of order and efficiency in transportation and industry, it will be a great educational instrument—none the less because it achieves its purpose without the effort or even the consciousness of the citizen.[11]

A journalistic popularization of the Regional Plan concludes:

If it is a good plan it will command popular interest, and if it commands sufficient popular interest over a long enough period of time it will be carried out.[12]

Although this alternative of a purely technical role for RPA was consistent with some expressions of planning doctrine, few if any of the early participants fully subscribed to it. McAneny, RPA's first president, was a particularly outspoken critic of this narrow conception of RPA's mission. Citing the many jurisdictions in the region, he said:

So with some 350 projects in the Plan, half a dozen or more separate bodies must take action to carry out each one of them. In short, carrying out the Regional Plan means the right action by the right people at the right time.

Will all this just happen fortuitously, making steady progress

possible? Of course it will not. It must be made to happen. That
is the primary objective of the Regional Plan Association.[13]

Speaking of RPA's educational and research efforts, he continued:

All this work is tremendously valuable; not that it will in itself
speedily result in carrying out the Plan, because it will not; but
because it is fundamental contributory work. . . . By itself, it does
not go far enough—or more accurately, it does not go fast enough;
but as part of a unified scheme of attack it is basic and therefore
invaluable.[14]

Though most of RPA's leaders shared McAneny's view that
something beyond research and education was necessary, his
making these statements may indicate some tendencies within
RPA toward a very circumscribed role.

At the other extreme, the nature of the Regional Plan itself
suggested an alternative leadership strategy, to commit RPA
to a crusade for metropolitan government. Although some may
have regarded this alternative as a theoretically ideal solution,
it was generally viewed as highly impractical and far too long-
range for the implementation of the Regional Plan and was
rejected.

The very existence of the Regional Plan attests to the belief
that significant action on the regional level is possible. If such
action does not follow automatically from the existence of the
Plan and if a governmental structure is not sought, how is it
to be brought about? At a minimum going just one step beyond the self-executing-plan view, establishment of official
planning agencies throughout the region was necessary. The
Regional Plan, RPA's constitution, and the work of the promotional staff of the Committee could all be cited in support of
this. The RPA constitution could be interpreted as viewing a
good plan plus official agencies as a sufficient condition for carrying out the Plan. To stop here, however, would be to assume
that the existence of the administrative machinery would be
enough to assure that that machinery would work, and for the

proper objectives. Many of RPA's early leaders were not willing to make such a mechanistic assumption.

McAneny advocated supplementing good plans and official agencies with a low-pressure role of direct personal contact with relevant public officials. This role would have RPA hovering on the fringes of the region's political processes, keeping abreast of developments, and quietly intervening when a propitious situation was presented. McAneny spelled this out in a memorandum on "Cooperation with Public Officials":

With its knowledge of what is going on in the region, with its technical grasp of the Regional Plan in detail, with its eye on planning activities not only hereabouts but elsewhere in the country, the Association has much to offer. . . . This work . . . means quietly and patiently making friends, gauging personalities, understanding political situations, sensing just what can be done and what can't be done. . . . [RPA's] place is properly in the background, for good reasons; and it will continue to follow this policy.[15]

McAneny viewed this as a mild political action role, based on quiet contact and persuasion and relying on the intelligence and skills that RPA possessed and the status positions and leadership skills of its leaders.

McAneny believed in making greater use of RPA's officers and directors as a leadership resource than did those who were more technically oriented. All agreed on the role of the board as a badge of organizational status, as the "legitimizing" sponsor of RPA plans, and as a channel to funds. McAneny also intended to use the board as a means of access to key decision-makers. Hence, it was important to bring together on the RPA board a regional elite for both practical and symbolic purposes. McAneny explained the need to recruit such an elite in an early memorandum to the directors:

There has been a direct attack on the problems of organizing strong citizen support for planning activities in general and for the Regional Plan in particular. The distinction between "strong citizen support" and support of the citizenry in general is important. To illustrate: the adoption in 1916 of the zoning ordinance in New

York involved no bond issue, nothing that required the support of the general public to advance. What was required was the concentrated support of a few people who really counted and it was such support that eventually made the zoning ordinance an accomplished fact. Much that is important in the Regional Plan can be carried out similarly. It is not necessary always that thoughtful, progressive citizens wait for the rest to catch up before action can be taken.[16]

This was an elaboration of Norton's view of organizing planning around the sponsorship of leading "public-spirited" citizens. There was no articulate sentiment for a more vigorous role of political leadership than the cautious, restrained conception of McAneny.

Throughout RPA's history there have been periodic tensions between technical and activist conceptions of RPA's role. From the beginning, some members of the staff, engrossed in the actual preparation of plans and conduct of research, have consciously or unconsciously tended toward a predominantly technical orientation. Some other staff members and some directors, especially those with experience in government or public administration have favored a more vigorous role along the lines suggested by McAneny. Such differences have usually been questions of degree rather than explicit "either-or" choices. Few of the technically oriented have consistently advocated a self-fulfilling plan viewpoint. The "activists" likewise have viewed a well-researched program as a necessary focus for organizing regional leadership. The question generally has been how far RPA should go in exercising a leadership role and what priorities should be established for allocation of organizational resources. McAneny and a few others wanted to put research and leadership functions roughly on a par. Until very recently, most participants would not have gone quite that far. Virtually no one, however, has questioned the desirability of at least a modest action commitment; it is the matter of degree and extent that has been controversial.

The primacy of a "planning" orientation over an "action"

orientation in the beginning and the implications of such planning doctrine tended to make the leadership commitment a subordinate one. This tendency was reinforced by the region's diffuse and unstructured political environment. Yet it was precisely because of this environment that the leadership commitment was crucial. An extraordinary amount of skills and resources was necessary to effectuate even a mild political action role in this environment. In the light of RPA's subsequent history, it seems possible that the early leaders, far-sighted though they were, underestimated the magnitude of the task of organizing regional leadership.

Selection of a Social Base

The selection and recruitment of participants and sponsors of an organization is one of the critical decision phases experienced early in a group's history and one that significantly affects its future course of development. A group such as RPA, whose goals are relatively abstract and intangible, has a special need to recruit a community elite at least nominally committed to their values. This kind of sponsorship serves a "legitimizing" function, conferring a degree of status to an enterprise, and also provides a tangible base of support among some of the social and economic structures of status and influence in the community.

RPA inherited the experience of the Committee on the Regional Plan. From the beginning, Norton had envisioned the Plan being made under the sponsorship of a distinguished group of leading citizens. The Committee was the prototype for RPA. It had been composed of a small number of civic-minded patricians who had an inbred sense of civic obligation and who sought to live up to an ideal of disinterested public service—an aristocracy in the best sense of the term. It was assumed that the RPA board would be made up of similar types.

It was also thought necessary to achieve some geographical balance among the various parts of the region on the RPA board. The Committee on the Regional Plan had been an almost entirely Manhattan-based group. Geographical balance was thought to be more important for carrying out the Plan and maintaining a going organization than for the initial task of supervising the making of the Plan.

RPA's goal, therefore, was to recruit persons of high status in both social and economic spheres who were interested in planning and civic leadership and to achieve as far as possible balanced representation of various parts of the region.

Some critics of the Regional Plan apparently interpreted this kind of commitment as a symptom of "vested interest" bias. Lewis Mumford, writing in the *New Republic,* stated that the plan

was conceived first of all in terms which would meet the interests and prejudices of the existing financial rulers: indeed, the very project was conceived and sponsored originally by enlightened members of this caste, and its aim, from the beginning, was as much human welfare and amenity as could be obtained without altering any of the political or business institutions which have made the city precisely what it is.[17]

One of RPA's present-day leaders observed that the planners of the 1920s had perhaps left themselves open for charges of "vested interests" because of some of their conceptions of planning. The Regional Plan was based on the value judgments of "experts" (planners) concerning the social and esthetic goals to be embodied in the region's growth pattern:

The community was presented with the physical conclusions, and was asked to take the value choices underlying those conclusions at face value. There was no effort to involve various community interests in considerations of alternative goals that might have been embodied in the Plan.

The defect, therefore, was not a corruption of the Plan by a nebulous elite conspiracy, but an overconfident commitment to technical expertise and a belief in the inherent rationality of a well-developed plan. RPA's perennially precarious financial condition also casts doubt on the suggestion of elite bias. RPA's commitment was simply to recruit as distinguished and as committed a group of "public-spirited citizens" from throughout the region as possible.

CORPORATE PARTICIPANTS

A substantial majority of RPA's directors have come from the upper echelons of the business and financial community (Table 1 at the end of this chapter). RPA has preferred to enlist major company presidents and board chairmen wherever possible. Because of the time pressures of highly responsible executive positions and the keen competition for the civic energies of such figures, this has often been a difficult task. RPA has been at least moderately successful in recruiting directors of the desired status.

Of RPA's 144 directors (1929–63) 142 have been identified: 93 of these have come from business and finance, and 58 of these were company presidents or board chairmen (25 of these coming on the board during its first five years), while 35 have been vice-presidents or middle-echelon executives. Many of these second- and middle-level executives come from major corporations whose vice-presidents would rank beside presidents of lesser concerns in status position.

RPA was particularly successful in its early years in attracting top corporate figures to its board. After the expansion of the board from 21 to 36 members in 1931, the board included the presidents of the New York Telephone Company, of the New York Edison Company (who was also president of six other power companies), of Western Electric, of New Jersey Bell Telephone, of the Public Service Gas and Electric Company of Newark, and of the National City Bank, the president of a bloc of twelve insurance companies, the board chairmen of Otis Elevator Company and R. H. Macy, leading figures in real estate and construction, and the head of the Macy newspaper chain.

RPA has not been quite so successful in later years; some of these concerns have been represented on the RPA board by vice-presidents since the retirement of these original board members. Nevertheless, RPA has enjoyed sustained support and representation from many of the major utilities and banks (and, to a lesser extent, insurance companies) and a few other large corporations prominent in the metropolitan region. Although the board has not always been of uniformly high status, RPA has probably been at least as successful as most civic organizations in recruiting such participants.

What incentives lead high-level executives, whose time is usually quite valuable, to join the RPA board? The members of the original Committee on the Regional Plan possessed many of the characteristics of some of the later participants, but they also were inspired by a zeal for planning greater than is likely to be encountered in the average corporate executive. Interviews with directors and staff members reveal at least two institutional incentives for corporate involvement in RPA— the direct relevance of RPA's research and the appropriateness of RPA for discharging some of the civic participation and philanthropic obligations attendant to high status.

Many of the corporations that form the hard core of RPA's consistent support claim to derive important research data from the Association. Data concerning trends of population, land use, home building, population density, and related matters are of direct importance to some kinds of businesses, especially those like utilities, which must make large investments for provision of services over a long period of time.

Some of the businesses benefiting from RPA's research functions operate either on a regional basis or a basis substantially broader than the boundaries of local political jurisdictions.

Since no official agency regularly collects and publishes data on a regional basis, RPA studies of regional development trends are an effective supplement to such a business' own research and planning operations.

Further, many of these businesses are in some sense "prisoners" of the region. Utilities, banks, insurance companies, and perhaps some large retail firms cannot flee the region and relocate elsewhere, as some industries can easily do. These firms have a greater stake in understanding and improving the region and perceive a more direct utility in RPA.

This motive for supporting RPA is not the only incentive for corporate participation, nor is it a primary inducement for many firms whose decisions are not so directly involved with regional trends. The large corporation in modern society is regarded as having an institutional responsibility to participate in selected civic and philanthropic enterprises for the sake of community relations. RPA has always been perceived as an appropriate instrument for fulfilling civic responsibilities by most of its board members. This is almost certainly at least a part of the motivation for participation of virtually all the corporate executives on the board.

RPA has strong competition in attempting to attract participants on this basis. In the New York region there is an almost infinite number of outlets for corporate civic virtue. Although RPA has had a fair measure of success in recruiting leading business and civic figures, it is by no means the only organization—or even one of a handful of organizations—appropriate for elite participation. Because of the size of the New York region, RPA probably has considerably more rivalry for the time and attention of potential board members than would be the case in a small or middle-sized metropolitan area.

The nature of RPA's concerns also poses a problem in recruiting support on a community relations basis. Since RPA's interests are relatively abstract and intangible, they do not always appear to be as immediately important as those of some other groups. It is easier for an executive to understand the concerns of, say, the Association for Improving the Condition of the Poor, the Municipal Art Society, the Metropolitan Opera Guild, or the Citizens Budget Commission than to grasp the essential unity of the twenty-two-county region and the significance of its planning problems. Consequently, if a direct economic stake in RPA's work is not perceived, it appears that some minimal indoctrination in the goals and values of regional planning is often necessary to enlist directors and to keep them involved. RPA thus has had problems of communicating its concerns to potential supporters that other high-status civic organizations have not shared.

These institutional inducements for corporate participation do not tell the whole story of why board members participate. From the beginning, factors of a personal nature have been keenly important. Many board members have consented to serve in part because they were solicited by a friend or associate committed to RPA. Directors are usually nominated from among acquaintances and colleagues of board members, especially the active core. There has always been, some observers report, a clublike quality to the board. Like most civic boards, the RPA directors have valued consensus and usually exercised some care to see that prospective members would fit in. This policy has usually meant more than a general acceptance of RPA's goals. It has involved being in some sense a social equal of the other members, a secure, settled figure who clearly does not need or wish to use the Association as an instrument for personal advancement. A consequence of this pattern of personal contact in recruitment has been that cohesion was maximized at the expense of keeping the board somewhat narrow, in that the types of persons on the board tended to reproduce themselves in recruiting new members.

A further result of these varying motives for participation should be noted. Since RPA is one of the acceptable avenues for discharging some of the civic responsibilities attached to

high status and since personal ties may play some part in recruitment, some members of RPA's board may have no more
than a minimal commitment to RPA's doctrinal goals and
values. It is possible that for some directors, their commitment
to planning goals may be less significant in their decision to
participate than these other incentives. It cannot be naturally
assumed, therefore, that all RPA's board members constitute
part of a nascent regional leadership; the regional focus may
not be a high-priority interest for at least some board members.

OTHER PARTICIPANTS

As indicated in Table 1, a substantial majority of RPA's
directors have come from the business world. Seventeen more
have been lawyers, many of whom have had close ties with the
top levels of the business and financial worlds. The largest remaining category of directors is composed of technical profes-
sionals—engineers, architects, and planners. Seventeen directors
have come from these backgrounds.

Among these, the community relations incentive has doubtless played some part. Many of these technicians, however, have
been attracted to RPA by their interest in its research and
techniques and by the esthetic appeal of planning. RPA, especially in its early years, was staffed largely by engineers and
architects turned planners. There was thus a common technical
and professional background which made RPA highly interest-
ing and a particularly appropriate outlet for civic participation
for these directors.

Although it is arguable that the commitment of these pro-
fessionals to RPA's planning goals may have been more deeply
ingrained than among some of the corporate participants, this
type of professional interest in RPA has also been an inducement for some of the corporate figures on the board. Some of
these, although recruited from the management circles of large
corporations, were originally trained in engineering or related
fields.

The remaining directors include several educators, three

women philanthropists, and a labor official. A retired public official and one other appointed public official from an academic background round out the group. No professional politician has been on RPA's board, although a number of attorneys and others with considerable experience in public affairs have served.

THE ACTIVE MINORITY

The phenomenon of the active minority, or activist core, in organizations has been frequently noted.[18] This condition is found in RPA as in most other civic groups. Attendance at board meetings is seldom higher than 50 percent and is frequently well below. Actual leadership is exercised by a small core of active directors, along with key members of the staff. Long-time participants say that the best approximation of the activist core is RPA's executive committee, composed of its officers and a few key directors. This committee makes most important policy decisions, subject to ratification by the full board, and it is in its meetings that the most thorough and candid discussions of policy issues takes place.

The executive committee has varied in size from 6 to 15 members at various times. Its present membership is 12. The committee is appointed by the Association president, usually after consultation with top members of the staff. A total of 45 directors have served on this body from 1929 to the present.

Considerable continuity has been maintained on the executive committee. The average tenure of members is 6.1 years (including all members of the present committee, 5 of whom have been appointed in the last five years); 10 have served ten years or more; 18 have served less than three years (including 4 members of the present committee). Only 13 members served on this body prior to 1941; 3 of these (Lawson Purdy, George McAneny, and Henry James) had been members of the Committee on the Regional Plan. RPA has thus been continuously linked with its past, and the roster of executive committee members, particularly of those who have served longer terms, provides an identification of RPA's activists. It could perhaps be assumed that some indication of where the strongest interests in RPA's regional commitments lie could be gleaned from this roster (Table 2 at the end of this chapter).

GEOGRAPHICAL REPRESENTATION

RPA's commitment to bring together a regionwide elite on its board required the recruitment of leaders from the various sectors of the metropolitan area. The original board, like the Committee on the Regional Plan, was largely a central-city group. Of its 20 members (the twenty-first member resigned within two weeks of his election), 14 were residents of New York City, 2 resided in the New York counties outside New York City, and 4 were New Jersey residents. There were no Connecticut residents on the original board.

Over time, RPA has overcome the initial preponderance of central-city residents. The residences of 126 of RPA's 144 directors at the time of their election have been determined: 50 have been from New York City, 27 from the New York area outside New York City, 35 from New Jersey, and 14 from Connecticut. Although many of those residing outside New York City had primary business interests in the central city, RPA has usually assumed that place of residence is a sufficient basis for achieving geographical balance on the board. On the other hand, some of the non-central-city residents had substantial business interests in the region outside New York City. This has been particularly true of many directors chosen from New Jersey.

Roughly the same geographical distribution has prevailed on the executive committee. Forty-one of the 45 members of this committee since 1929 could be located: of these 19 resided in New York City, 9 in New York outside New York City, 11 in New Jersey, and 2 in Connecticut.

In summary, RPA's commitment to create a board of leading citizens of the region has been at least partially implemented.

While the RPA board at any given time has not quite measured up to the Committee on the Regional Plan in terms of status, it has remained a relatively high-status group throughout most of its history. It has expanded from a primarily central-city base to more balanced regional distribution of directors.

This is a considerable achievement. RPA, aiming high, has encountered great competition for the time and attention of high-level executives. A long-time leader of RPA, who has approached numerous prospects for service on RPA's board over many years' time, has reported that RPA is turned down about 50 percent of the time. In view of its aspirations and the relative abstractness of its concerns, RPA's record of leadership recruitment must be termed at least a qualified success.[19]

RPA, then, inherited a set of commitments to doctrines stressing comprehensive physical planning of the entire metropolitan region and expressing high confidence in the coordinative and educational qualities of good plans. These inherited doctrines were an ambiguous legacy with respect to strategies for implementing plans. At the same time, RPA was committed to the recruitment of an elite group of regional civic and business leaders to serve on its board, providing status and leadership resources. Attention is now directed to the working out of these commitments in RPA's early program and the ensuing consequences for RPA's role as a regional leadership institution.

TABLE 1

DIRECTORS OF THE
REGIONAL PLAN ASSOCIATION, 1929–63

Name	Occupation
	1929
William D. Baldwin	Board chairman, Otis Elevator Co.
Alexander M. Bing	Bing & Bing, Inc. (real estate)
Edgar S. Bloom	President, Western Electric Co.

Name	*Occupation*
Henry L. de Forest	Vice-president, counsel, and director, Hackensack Water Co.; Spring Valley Water Works & Supply Co.
John H. Finley	Associate editor, N.Y. *Times*
John M. Glenn	General director, Russell Sage Foundation
Shelby M. Harrison	Director, Dept. of Surveys and Exhibits, Russell Sage Foundation
Wayne Heydecker	Planner
Henry James	Attorney, writer
Frederick P. Keppel	President, Carnegie Corp.
George McAneny	Attorney, public official
Charles G. Meyer	Real estate
Garrison Norton	Attorney (son of Charles D. Norton)
Grover O'Neill	President, Grover O'Neill & Co. (investment banking)
Lawrence M. Orton	Planner
E. H. Outerbridge	President, Harvey & Outerbridge; Pantasote Leather Co.; Agasote Millboard Co.
Frank L. Polk	Attorney
J. Kingsley Powell	Vice-president, N.J. Association of Real Estate Boards
Frederic B. Pratt	Partner, Charles Pratt & Co.; president, Morris Building Co.; president, Pratt Institute
Lawson Purdy	Attorney
Frank H. Quinby	Architect (president, N.Y. State Association of Architects)
Daniel S. Sanford	Headmaster, Sanford School, Redding Ridge, Conn.
Bertram H. Saunders	President, Hohokus Bleachery (piece-goods finishing)
Flavel Shurtleff	Planner
Robert E. Simon	Real estate (president and director of 7 firms)
Percy S. Straus	Board chairman, R. H. Macy & Co.
Earle Talbot	Vice-president, Hackensack Water Co.
Dewitt Van Buskirk	Banker

1931 (expansion of board)

Chester I. Barnard	President, N.J. Telephone Co.
Franklin Q. Brown	President, Dobbs Ferry (N.Y.) Bank, Colony Realty Corp., Newberry Corp.
Thomas Crimmins	President, Thomas Crimmins Contracting Co.
Johnston de Forest	Attorney
Lee J. Eastman	President, Packard Motor Car Co. of N.Y.
Wilfred Kurth	Insurance executive (president of 12 companies)
Thomas N. McCarter	President, Public Service Gas & Electric Co. of N.J. (Newark)
James S. McCulloh	President, N.Y. Telephone Co.
Edward A. MacDougall	President, Queensboro Corp. (developer of Jackson Heights)
J. Noel Macy	Publisher and general manager, Westchester Publications, Inc.
Mrs. Charles D. Norton	Philanthropist

Name	Occupation
Mrs. Harold Pratt	Philanthropist (sister-in-law of Frederic B. Pratt)
Gordon S. Rentschler	President, National City Bank of N.Y.
Matthew S. Sloan	President, N.Y. Edison Co.
William Ziegler, Jr.	President, Royal Baking Powder Co.

1932

George A. Brownell	Attorney
Eli W. Debevoise	Attorney
Darwin R. James	President, East River Savings Bank
Walter Kidde	President, Walter Kidde & Co.; Walter Kidde Constructors
Orrin C. Lester	Vice-president, Bowery Savings Bank
J. Spencer Smith	Board chairman, County Trust Co., Bergen County

1935–39

Henry Bruere	President, Bowery Savings Bank
Harvey W. Corbett	Architect
George W. Farny	Highway engineer
Frederick C. Horner	Assistant to the chairman, General Motors Corp.
Kenneth Ives	Real estate
Mrs. William Ladd	Philanthropist
Edward J. Mathews	Architect
George W. Merck	President, Merck & Co. (manufacturing chemists)
William C. Moore	Retired (former member of Federal Resettlement Administration)
C. McKim Norton	Attorney (later executive vice-president of RPA)
Harold S. Osborne	Chief Engineer, American Telephone & Telegraph Co.
Alfred H. Swayne	Board chairman, General Motors Corp.
William S. Weeks	. . .*
John Wilkie	Vice-president and treasurer, Central Hudson Gas & Electric Co. (Poughkeepsie)

1940–44

James Byrne	Attorney; chancellor, State University of N.Y.; president, N.Y. City Bar Assn.
Robert W. Dowling	President, City Investing Co. (real estate)
Louis I. Dublin	Second vice-president and statistician, Metropolitan Life Insurance Co.
Gano Dunn	Engineer; director, Radio Corp. of America; National Broadcasting Co.
Thomas S. Holden	President, F. W. Dodge Co. (construction)
George LeBoutillier	Vice-president, Pennsylvania and Long Island Railroads
Ralph Peters, Jr.	President, Corn Exchange Bank & Trust Co.
R. R. Rogers	Vice-president, Prudential Insurance Co.
Bayard Schiefflin	President, Cargo Marine Coal & Shipping Co. (exporters)

* Unknown.

Name	*Occupation*
Earl B. Schwulst	President, Bowery Savings Bank
John S. Sinclair	Attorney
Henry Steinmetz	. . .*
David L. Tilley	President, N.Y. Dock Co.
Delos Walker	Vice-president, R. H. Macy & Co.
Paul Windels	Attorney

1945–49

Walter Binger	Engineer
George L. Bliss	President, Century Federal Savings & Loan Assn.
Henry J. Davenport	President, Home Title Guaranty Co. (real estate)
Harris A. Dunn	Vice-chairman, Bowery Savings Bank
Alexander H. Elder	General solicitor, Jersey Central Railroad
Lurelle Guild	President, Lurelle Guild Associates (industrial design)
Clarence L. Law	Vice-president, Consolidated Edison Co.
Thomas N. McCarter, Jr.	Executive vice-president, Public Service Gas & Electric Co. of N.J.
Edwin I. Marks	Director, R. H. Macy & Co.
William L. Maude	President, Howard Savings Institution (Newark)
Otto L. Nelson	Vice-president, N.Y. Life Insurance Co.
Alfred Rheinstein	President, Rheinstein Construction Co.
Robert C. Richter	Attorney
George F. Smith	President, Johnson & Johnson (pharmaceuticals)
William E. Speers	President, James McCutcheon & Co. (department store)
Gardner W. Taylor	President, First Federal Savings & Loan Assn.
George S. Van Schaick	Attorney
Stephen F. Voorhees	Architect
George C. Waldo	President and editor-in-chief, Bridgeport *Post*

1950–54

Leland Bonnett	Vice-president, Consolidated Edison Co.
James W. Carpenter	Vice-president, Long Island Lighting Co.; Queensborough Gas & Electric Co.
Willard G. Hampton	Executive vice-president, N.Y. Telephone Co.
Sherman R. Hoyt	Industrialist (retired)
John Kidde	President, Walter Kidde Construction Co.
Joseph E. McClean	Conservation Commissioner, State of N.J.
Henry K. Norton	President, N.Y., Susquehanna & Western (Erie) Railroad
H. Bruce Palmer	President, Mutual Benefit Life Insurance Co. (Newark)
Orville H. Schell	Attorney
H. C. Turner, Jr.	President, Turner Construction Co.
Walter L. Weil	President, Commercial Factors Corp.

* Unknown.

1955-59

Name	Occupation
Max Abramovitz	Architect
Amory H. Bradford	Vice-president and business manager, N.Y. *Times*
Edwin S. Burdell	President, Cooper Union
Ralph W. Crolly	Attorney
Thomas J. Deegan, Jr.	President, Thomas J. Deegan Co. (construction)
James Fairman	Vice-president, Consolidated Edison Co.
Paul H. Folwell	Attorney
Luther H. Gulick	President, Institute of Public Administration
Joseph Kaiser	President, Williamsburgh Savings Bank
John W. Larsen	Executive vice-president and treasurer, Bowery Savings Bank
Otto W. Manz, Jr.	Executive vice-president, Consolidated Edison Co.
Albert Mayer	Architect
Frank C. Moore	President, Government Affairs Foundation
A. R. Nelson	Vice-president, Public Service Gas & Electric Co. (Newark)
Ralph Paine, Jr.	Vice-president, *Time,* Inc.; publisher, *Architectural Forum*
Elmo Roper	Marketing consultant
Louis Sachar	President, Marshall Management Corp.
James S. Schoff	President, Bloomingdale Bros.
Milford A. Vieser	Financial vice-president, Mutual Benefit Life Insurance Co.
Howard B. Wakeman	Vice-president, Long Island Lighting Co.
Ralph Walker	Architect

1960-63

Cowles Andrus	Vice-chairman, N.J. Bank & Trust Co. (retired)
Cesar J. Bertheau	President, People's Trust Co. of Bergen County (Hackensack)
Charles F. Bound	Vice-president, Morgan Guaranty Trust Co.
Charles A. Cronheim	Vice-president, R. H. Macy & Co.
Percy L. Douglas	President, Otis Elevator Co.
Frederick H. Groel	Executive vice-president, Prudential Insurance Co.
Mason Gross	President, Rutgers University
Arthur B. Langlie	President, McCall Corp.
Albert Merck	Investment executive
William S. Renchard	President, Chemical Bank N.Y. Trust Co.
George A. Roeder, Jr.	Executive vice-president, Chase Manhattan Bank
Wallace S. Sayre	Eaton Professor of Public Administration, Columbia University
Perry Coke Smith	Architect
Harry Van Arsdale, Jr.	President, N.Y. City Central Labor Council
Paul Windels, Jr.	Attorney
David L. Yunich	President, Macy's New York

Summary

Business:			
Banking	21	Lawyers	17
Utilities	18	Architects	8
Merchants	7	Planners	4
Manufacturers	12	Engineers	5
Newspapers and publishing	6	Education and research	9
Construction and real estate	16	Public officials	2
Insurance	8	Philanthropists	3
Shipping	1	Labor	1
Railroads	3	Unknown	2
Investments	1		
Total business	93		

TABLE 2
MEMBERS OF THE REGIONAL PLAN ASSOCIATION EXECUTIVE COMMITTEE

Year Appointed	Name	Occupation	Tenure, Years	Residence
1930	W. D. Baldwin	Manufacturer	1	New York City
	Alexander Bing	Real estate	6	New York City
	Henry James	Attorney	6	New York City
	George McAneny	Attorney	17	New York City
	Charles Meyer	Real estate	10	New York City
	Lawson Purdy	Attorney	12	New York City
	Bertram Saunders	Manufacturer	1	New Jersey
1931	Wayne Heydecker	Planner	1	Westchester
	Garrison Norton	Attorney	8	New York City
1935	Orrin Lester	Banker	2	Hartsdale, N.Y.
	Earle Talbot	Utility	5	New Jersey
1938	Mrs. William Ladd	Philanthropist	5	New York City
	Edward Mathews	Architect	3	. . .*
1941	John M. Glenn	Director, Russell Sage Foundation	9	New York City
	Thomas Holden	Construction	12	Darien, Conn.
	Frederick Horner	Engineer	1	. . .*
	Kenneth Ives	Real estate	2	Bedford Village, N.Y.
	Walter Kidde	Construction	2	Montclair, N.J.
	George W. Merck	Manufacturer	7	West Orange, N.J.
	William C. Moore	Administrator (retired)	1	. . .*
	C. McKim Norton †	Attorney	19	Princeton, N.J.
	Harold S. Osborne †	Engineer	22	Montclair, N.J.

* Undetermined.

Year Appointed	Name	Occupation	Tenure, Years	Residence
1943	Earl Schwulst	Banker	8	Southport, Conn.
	Delos Walker	Retailer	7	East Hampton, N.Y.
	Paul Windels	Attorney	14	New York City
1950	Walter Binger †	Engineer	14	New York City
	Gano Dunn	Engineer	6	New York City
	William Speers	Retailer	5	Montclair, N.J.
	George Van Schaick	Attorney	3	Bronxville, N.Y.
1953	Leland Bonnett	Utility	2	. . .*
	Otto L. Nelson	Insurance	10	Princeton, N.J.
1955	Willard G. Hampton †	Utility	9	Manhasset, N.Y.
	John Wilkie	Utility	2	Katonah, N.Y.
1956	John Larsen †	Banker	8	Haworth, N.J.
1957	Luther Gulick †	President, Institute of Public Administration	7	New York City
1958	Ralph Walker	Architect	1	Chappaqua, N.Y.
1959	Amory Bradford †	Publisher	7	New York City
	Edwin S. Burdell	Educator	1	New York City
1960	James Schoff †	Retailer	4	New York City
1961	Orville Schell	Attorney	1	New York City
1962	Cesar Bertheau	Banker	2	Mahwah, N.J.
1963	Max Abramovitz †	Architect	1	New York City
	George F. Smith †	Manufacturer	1	Metuchen, N.J.
	Otto Manz †	Utility	1	Rockville Center, N.Y.
	Perry Coke Smith †	Architect	1	New York City

* Undetermined.
† Member of 1964 Executive Committee.

CHAPTER III

Early Successes
and Their Consequences

Never in RPA's history has it had a program so specific, well-documented, and comprehensive as it had in the beginning. Its program consisted of the 470 recommended projects in the Regional Plan, each of which could be defended in terms of an integrated, comprehensive scheme of regional development.

To follow up and implement this program, RPA brought together one of the outstanding planning staffs in the nation. Its first general director was George B. Ford, an architect turned city planner who had served as a planning consultant to the War Department and as president of the Federated National Societies on Planning and Parks. The staff's associate director was Wayne Heydecker, a planner from the Russell Sage staff who had been actively involved in the work of the Committee on the Regional Plan. Other staff members included Flavel Shurtleff, of the staff of the Committee on the Regional Plan and director of the Planning Foundation of America; Nathaniel S. Olds, also an officer of the Planning Foundation of America; Edward McKernon, who had been associated with the Regional Plan Committee; and other engineers, draftsmen, and technicians. W. Philip Shatts, who had been associated with the Russell Sage Foundation and the Regional Plan Committee, was designated field secretary and headed the promotional branch of the staff.

The staff was enlarged to twenty-five on April 1, 1932, when the Association formally merged with the Committee on the Regional Plan. Ford, the Association's general director, died in 1930 and was not officially replaced. McAneny took on direction of the engineering staff and continued in this capacity until appointed sanitation commissioner of New York in 1933. When the merger took place in 1932, Harold M. Lewis of the Committee staff was named chief engineer, and Lawrence Orton, formerly secretary to the Committee, became general secretary of the Association. Orton succeeded to active directorship of the staff in 1933 when McAneny became sanitation commissioner.[1]

The technical staff had two major tasks. The first was to continue making fact-finding surveys like those made prior to the development of the Regional Plan. George McAneny stated:

Not all of these facts can be kept literally up to date, but careful observation of passenger movement, motor vehicle registration, the growth of "riding habit," population, park acreage, and the like, have served both to check the continuing validity of our proposals and to suggest modifications in them.[2]

Early studies of this kind included revisions of population estimates based on analyses of 1930 census data and the first of a continuing series of detailed counts of persons and vehicles entering Manhattan south of 59th Street on an ordinary business day.

The other main task of the technical staff was maintenance of a set of "office record maps" to keep a detailed check on the progress of the Regional Plan. These included maps showing all the important projects developed in the Plan and others showing various proposed and actual developments and projects in the region. These maps made it possible to assess precisely the status of the Regional Plan at all times.[3]

The promotional wing of the staff was charged with the organization of support for the establishment of county and municipal planning throughout the region. For the first four to five years of RPA's existence, this was its major activity.

Leadership in Planning

To promote official planning, RPA's staff conducted probably the only extensive "grass-roots" operation in RPA's history. This was not an aberration from the commitment not to be a "mass" organization; these efforts were to be set up as independent local citizens' groups, not to enlist a mass membership in RPA:

Due to its great size and population, and the complexity of its physical and political structure, the New York Region offers certain difficulties to the formation of a unified organization of citizens for any purpose, especially for one so new and imperfectly understood as city planning.

After considerable experimentation and conference with local leaders, the Regional Plan Association formulated a plan of organization by means of which it might aid the local communities to develop planning programs and to organize citizen support for them, and at the same time lay the foundation for broad public support of the larger features of the Regional Plan.[4]

The organizational thrust here came from the top down. RPA staff and board members from the areas involved selected a "leading citizen" in each county who would act as chairman for the organization of county planning councils. This individual often turned out to be an RPA board member. He would then select leaders from each of the municipalities within his county, and they would constitute the planning council for that county. The local representatives were then to call on the various civic organizations in their communities to name representatives to local planning councils. This was an attempt to secure broad support for planning by mobilizing the leadership of existing organizations in the region. RPA viewed its role as a top-level regional elite stimulating civic interest in planning at successively lower levels of government.

Much of the success of the movement would depend on RPA's ability to recruit the type of leadership its self-conception called for.

RPA was active in all seventeen counties in the region outside New York City. By 1933 planning councils at the county level existed in ten of the seventeen counties and 252 existed at the municipal level.[5] RPA supplied these groups with a Community Planning Manual, a how-to-do-it exposition of planning principles designed for laymen. It also published booklets describing the application of the Regional Plan to each individual county.

In most of the counties public meetings were arranged where RPA spokesmen presented the Plan's proposals for that county to the county governing board. In the meantime, RPA drafted state enabling bills for county planning that, with some important amendments, were enacted by the state legislature of New York (after an initial failure because of a gubernatorial veto). Similar legislation was supported in New Jersey, where limited success was eventually attained.[6]

RPA did not extend its planning council organizations to New York City. Here McAneny and other leaders had numerous contacts within the city government, and when Mayor O'Brien appointed an advisory committee on city planning in 1932, McAneny and Harold Lewis, chief engineer of the Association, were members. In 1934 Mayor La Guardia appointed a mayor's committee on city planning and consulted McAneny concerning its organization and functions. Percy S. Straus, Board Chairman of R. H. Macy and Company and an RPA director, was named to the Mayor's committee, as was Lewis. Lawrence Orton, general secretary of the Association, served as secretary and project director to the Mayor's committee. (He later became a charter member of the New York City Planning Commission.)[7] These established patterns of communication made the planning-council approach unnecessary in New York City.

RPA was thus trying to develop a structure of communication and influence that would help secure the execution of the Plan. The specificity of the Plan's recommendations, broken down by counties, gave the promotional staff a tangible product to sell. This was a low-pressure leadership role stressing the rationality of a good plan in the context of the sponsorship of a group of prestigious citizens.

By 1933, there were 8 official county planning boards in the region, and 109 municipal boards. Several parts of the Plan were being carried out, and other parts were officially adopted. Of the 51 proposals classified as "urgent" in the 1929 Plan, 15 had been carried out or were in the process of completion, and 13 others had been officially adopted by 1933. Of the highway mileage recommended by the Plan, 22 percent was constructed or under construction, and official commitments had been made to build 14 percent more.[8] It is not possible to attribute all these developments to the influence of the Regional Plan without risking a *post hoc* fallacy. The makers of the Plan did not claim complete originality. They readily admitted that many proposals were suggested or developed by others,[9] and it is possible that some of the recommendations anticipated choices already implicitly made. Nevertheless, in its first four years RPA could point to an impressive *prima facie* record of achievement. This record was perhaps all the more significant in view of depression conditions, which had caused almost all units of government to slow down spending for public projects.

The Stimulus of the New Deal

The coming of the depression created serious problems for RPA, especially in its fund-raising. It was impossible to raise the funds necessary for a self-sustaining operation. Only the continued financial support of the Russell Sage Foundation enabled RPA to survive. In other respects, however, the depression and the relief programs of the New Deal presented unusual opportunities for RPA.

Title II of the National Industrial Recovery Act of 1933 created the Public Works Administration, with broad powers to spend large sums for public works projects. The National Planning Board, composed of Frederic Delano, Charles Merriam, and Wesley Mitchell, was set up as an advisory body within the PWA. Delano, formerly chairman of the Committee on the Regional Plan, chaired the National Planning Board. Harold Ickes, administrator of the PWA, wanted, according to Arthur Schlesinger, Jr., "to beautify the national estate through the honest building of durable public monuments." [10] Whether through the influence of Delano's National Planning Board or through his own predilections, Ickes decided that projects proposed for PWA support should preferably be related to a broad master plan of comprehensive development. A similar decision was reached by Harry Hopkins' short-lived Civil Works Administration, which also stipulated that at least 3 percent of those on CWA work relief would be assigned to planning activities.[11] Both agencies would give preference to proposals explicitly related to master plans. These decisions, in which RPA's supporter Frederic Delano may have had a hand, proved to be a major windfall for RPA.

RPA overnight came to occupy a particularly strategic position. It possessed a ready-made series of proposals, all of which could be justified in terms of a larger master plan. Furthermore, county and city governments were aware of RPA and its program as a result of the extensive promotional activity conducted by the staff since 1929.

The Association originally limited itself to distributing to officials and influential citizens lists of projects for which federal funds might be sought, with explanations of how to apply and justify the proposals. As more federal funds became available and more communities sought aid, RPA had to take a more active role.[12] Many communities lacked funds to employ anyone qualified to direct the preliminary organization of projects and to draft the technical details of the proposals. RPA consequently abandoned its general policy of not providing direct technical assistance to local governments (a policy designed to prevent competition with private planners and consultants). A full-time staff member was added whose sole responsibility was to work on proposals for work relief projects. The Association participated in every phase of the preparation of these projects for a large number of the region's governmental units.

For two to three years, these projects were almost the sole activity of RPA. Detailed records were kept indicating the precise status of each project in which RPA was interested. Projects were followed from inception through local, district, and state channels, through the various steps of federal approval, then back down through channels involved in execution of the proposal. The technical competence of RPA assumed proportions of great importance, enhancing RPA's stature as well as facilitating the realization of many features of the 1929 Plan.

In connection with this activity, the creation of official planning agencies was pursued with renewed vigor. Communities wanted planning bodies which could approve proposals sent to Washington, a stimulus of some significance. By 1936 every county in the region had an official planning board. The activity of these boards ranged from approval of proposals submitted to Washington to fact-finding and research studies staffed mostly by men on relief. Between 1933 and 1936, "more than a million dollars had been spent and over a thousand men had been employed on detailed planning surveys and studies." [13] McAneny attributed most of this success in establishing planning to the federal decisions:

When the relief policies of state and nation made it evident that large numbers of the unemployed would be put to work on worthwhile projects, we saw an opportunity to advance our cause through county planning projects while, at the same time, rendering a distinct service to the unemployed. It is no exaggeration to say that, from that time on, organizing the counties for the promotion of planning projects, helping them to qualify for federal aid, and so establishing planning as an integral part of the county government, was the most important single activity of the Association; that it has been eminently successful; and principally, although by no means wholly, responsible for the happy state of affairs to which I referred when I said that planning was now an official matter in every one of our counties.[14]

A crowning achievement in official planning was the establishment of the New York City Planning Commission in 1938. The Association's leadership was actively involved in the preliminary staffwork and negotiations that led to this.

The charter of the New York City Planning Commission embodied most of RPA's conceptions of planning organization. The new commission was "looked to for the fullest demonstration of the potentialities of the semi-independent planning agency." [15] The commission was to be an expert body whose members served eight-year overlapping terms and could not be removed for "political" reasons. It was to prepare and keep up to date a master plan for the city and prepare both zoning regulations and the annual capital budget for the city, to be submitted to the Board of Estimate. The "expert" status of the commission was bolstered by the appointment of distinguished figures with some competence in planning who were more or less committed to the doctrine of expert independence from the usual pressures and influences of the political process.[16] Lawrence Orton of the RPA staff was one of the original members.

The National Planning Board also stimulated creation of state planning agencies. Wayne Heydecker, of the RPA staff, became a member of the New York State Planning Board. RPA's influence continued to grow. During this heyday of public works spending, McAneny could say with little exaggeration that "There are few, if any, major planning projects promulgated in the Region regarding which our engineering staff is not consulted." [17]

Addressing RPA's annual meeting in 1936, McAneny cited the construction of the Queens-Midtown Tunnel in accordance with the recommendations of the 1929 Plan as evidence of how the Plan was being carried out. The chairman of the Queens-Midtown Tunnel Authority wrote McAneny that, when the Authority requested federal loans and grants amounting to $58 million, "The Authority submitted the tunnel proposal of the Regional Plan for the reason that it represented studies far beyond the ability of the Authority to make within any reasonable period, and conclusions that were accepted as sound." [18] The Association was in a particularly strategic position to supply exactly what the New Deal agencies were looking for.

EFFECTS ON RPA

How did these developments affect RPA's commitments and role? One consequence was a noticeable decline in the role of the promotional staff. From 1933 on, it was increasingly overshadowed by the technicians. Large-scale promotion became less important, while the technical services of the Association were much in demand.

Some of the technical staff saw little justification for extensive promotional activities. RPA was being sought out, and projects were being selected because of their relation to a regional master plan. Although the earlier efforts of the promotional staff facilitated this trend, the Plan seemed to be almost self-executing.

Furthermore, the goals of the earlier promotional activity—establishment of official planning and carrying out the Regional Plan—were now proceeding apace. Now what would the promoters promote? For a time this wing of the staff adopted Clarence Perry's "neighborhood unit" concept, which had been developed in one of the survey volumes preceding the Regional

Plan and had been further elaborated in more recent studies sponsored by the Russell Sage Foundation. The neighborhood unit was broadly consistent with the Regional Plan and stressed the desirability of restructuring the city in a pattern of self-contained, relatively self-sufficient neighborhood units, in which most basic services and community facilities would be easily available. This would hopefully promote greater sense of community and provide certain amenities more conveniently. It was hoped that this principle might be applied in the large-scale rebuilding of blighted areas.[19]

The neighborhood unit concept was more abstract and less immediately relevant to the planning activities going on in the region than were the physical recommendations of the Regional Plan. Over time, then, the promotional staff became increasingly isolated from the mainstream of RPA's operations. The rift that some observers assert had always existed to some degree between the promoters and the technicians widened, and the technicians became more and more the dominant force within the organization.

An important related consequence was the reinforcement of existing predilections to emphasize the purely physical aspects of planning. Federal funds were being given mainly for public works engineering projects. Thus, the RPA staff became almost exclusively concerned with engineering matters. Their own professional bent and the requirements of the situation pushed them in this direction. RPA's conception of planning became, in effect, narrowed to public works development. The *Annual Report* issued in 1934 states that, although planning has economic and social implications,

We are thinking of it primarily as *a process for contributing to the better physical development of the community, particularly as respects those permanent improvements that are paid for out of public funds.*[20] [Italics in the original.]

This is a retreat from the conception of planning developed by the Regional Plan.

In short, the circumstances of the 1930s brought about an increasingly technical orientation and dominance, reinforcement of a physical and engineering emphasis, and a consequent isolation of the promotional staff. These developments raised problems for the implementation of RPA's leadership commitment. The very conditions that brought about many of RPA's achievements obviated the necessity for sustained attention to the development of a leadership role, which was not a solidly entrenched commitment at any time. If unchecked, these conditions could be expected to facilitate the decline of RPA's leadership role.

The Assertion of Leadership

The active promotion of the Regional Plan in the 1930s brought the Association into contact with several of the principal governmental units in the region. Its closest contacts were probably with the city administration in New York, especially after La Guardia became mayor. Friendships between RPA leaders and members of the La Guardia administration enhanced RPA's access to the city government. Veteran observers have remarked that one important reason for the execution of several of the Plan proposals was the "favorable administrative climate" of the La Guardia administration. La Guardia accepted and supported the creation of the City Planning Commission, with which RPA was closely linked.

McAneny was consulted by state officials concerning the organization and staffing of the State Planning Board and other relevant state agencies, and the Association had, through Frederic Delano, access to major federal officials involved in public works spending and other planning-related activities.

Within the region, two great operations that Wood terms "metropolitan giants" [21] were emerging. The Port of New York Authority had not been notably successful during the 1920s in its efforts to coordinate railroad transportation but gained a new vigor with the great popularity of automobile transportation in the 1930s.[22] The Port Authority became involved in constructing and operating such automobile-oriented facilities as the George Washington Bridge and other river crossings and bus and marine terminals. The Authority prospered with the increased preference for the automobile and, in turn, probably contributed to that preference. Both the Authority's resurgence and the early completion of most of the highway proposals of the Regional Plan were symptomatic of the same emerging transportation preferences. The rail rapid transit proposals of the Regional Plan languished.

The Port Authority and RPA have generally enjoyed friendly and cordial relations. Two of RPA's original board members, E. H. Outerbridge and Dewitt Van Buskirk, had served on the Port Authority board. The two organizations found themselves on the same side of several important planning questions in the 1930s. Although they have not consistently agreed on all matters of transportation policy in subsequent years, they have continued to enjoy generally good relations and fairly close contact.

RPA was less successful in establishing a pattern of friendly relations with the other emerging metropolitan giant, the complex of agencies and authorities presided over by Robert Moses. Wood says that "no figure has better exemplified the special brand of Regional-enterprise politics—a high degree of executive and diplomatic skill blended expertly with a genius for keeping in the public eye" [23] than Moses. Moses became chairman of the Triborough Bridge Authority (later the Triborough Bridge and Tunnel Authority), with a sphere of jurisdiction over East River crossings roughly similar to the Port Authority's concentration on trans-Hudson development. He was also president of the Long Island State Park Commission and the Jones Beach State Parkway Authority and later became New York City Park Commissioner and City Construction coordinator. His state jobs included chairmanship of the

State Power Authority and the State Council of Parks. Obviously Moses, wearing many administrative hats simultaneously, was in a particularly strategic position to influence regional planning developments. His administrative empire did not grow to its full dimensions until the 1940s and 1950s but was being actively built up during the 1930s.

Moses and RPA were at odds from the outset. In the early 1930s, RPA opposed Moses' plans for constructing the Northern State Parkway. Moses, in turn, denounced the Regional Plan as "visionary" and its makers as "irresponsible." [24] Another clash occurred in 1938, when RPA opposed some of the Triborough Authority's parkway plans for the East Bronx. This time Moses stated in a letter released to the press that "The fact of the matter is they do not know what they are talking about and that there is no talent on the Regional Plan at the moment worth listening to or bothering about." [25]

Relations between RPA and Moses became more strained in 1939, when McAneny led the Association in one of its rare open political engagements. This incident provides not only understanding of the breach left between RPA and Moses but also some understanding of the nature of RPA's leadership role and the conditions and consequences of its utilization.

THE BATTERY BRIDGE CONTROVERSY

The Triborough Authority, headed by Moses, proposed in 1939 to construct a bridge spanning the East River between the Battery in Manhattan and Hamilton Avenue in Brooklyn at a cost of more than $41 million. The City Planning Commission, in line with recommendations of the Regional Plan, had earlier proposed a vehicular tunnel at that site but now reversed itself and endorsed Moses' bridge proposal.

RPA opposed this proposal for several reasons. The Regional Plan had recommended that all future river crossings connecting with southern Manhattan be tunnels rather than bridges. RPA regarded the site as a poor one for a bridge, believing that unnecessary defacement of the Battery Park area would result, which in turn would make impossible improvements of Battery Park contemplated in the Regional Plan. Although the Plan was revised in 1937 to include a tunnel at that location, RPA saw this as a matter of more local than regional significance and as a relatively low-priority project.[26] The bridge proposal was supported by various civic interests in Brooklyn, and it appeared likely to be accepted.

In February, 1939, the RPA board went on record in opposition to the bridge, and a resolution was adopted for presentation to the City Planning Commission and to the district engineer of the War Department, which had to approve the project. Without specific authorization from the Board, though undoubtedly after informal consultation with key members, McAneny organized an association of twenty-one civic and business organizations to oppose the bridge proposal.[27] The chairman and vice-chairman of the Central Committee of Organizations Opposing the Battery Bridge came from the Citizens Union and the West Side Association of Commerce, respectively, but it was McAneny who did most of the organizational work to bring this group together.

At the local level the Committee was unsuccessful; the proposal was endorsed by the City Council and by the Board of Estimate. The Committee, and RPA in particular, succeeded in arousing Moses' ire: in the hearings before the City Council, Moses called McAneny "an extinct volcano who never expects to run for public office again." [28] The Triborough Authority issued two pamphlets ridiculing the proposals in the Regional Plan for improvement of Battery Park,[29] indicating that Moses regarded RPA as his chief adversary among the organizations opposing his plan. This opposition accomplished little more than ruffling Moses; the Board of Estimate approved the bridge with only one dissenting vote.

The spokesmen of McAneny's civic committee appeared at the hearing set by the district engineer of the War Department.

There was apparently a feeling that the district engineer was not sympathetic to the committee's arguments, so McAneny, two days after the hearing, wrote to President Roosevelt and directed Harold Lewis, head of the RPA staff, to write Frederic Delano about the situation. Delano, head of the National Planning Board since 1933, had argued RPA's case before War Department officials before. War Department rulings had blocked plans to build a trans-Hudson bridge at 57th Street in Manhattan. Delano was advised of the Battery bridge issue and was asked to present RPA's case to the Secretary of War.

Six weeks later, the Secretary of War turned down the bridge proposal on the grounds that it might create a menace to navigation in time of war.[30] It has not been possible to document the role, if any, of Delano in this decision. It can be assumed, at the least, that RPA's cause was not damaged by having a friend in court. For whatever reasons, RPA was successful at the very top level of decision.

According to McAneny's *Reminiscences,* "Moses was very much enraged." [31] After this episode, close relationships between RPA and the agencies headed by Moses were frequently not possible. The agencies forming the "Moses empire" have therefore seldom come within RPA's orbit of influence, cutting RPA off from an important set of institutions with considerable power to affect the physical development of the region.

INTERNAL CONSEQUENCES

In the fight over the Battery bridge, McAneny was trying to make the most of RPA's potentialities as a leadership institution relying on high status and low-pressure political action. Other participants in RPA, however, were not as strongly committed to such a role.

The inevitable questions arose in the RPA board. This was probably the first occasion where the latent differences within the board concerning appropriate strategies of action came into the open. Although the board had passed a resolution opposing the bridge, it had not specifically authorized McAneny's involvement in the politics of the issue. At the first board meeting after the various public hearings on the issue, the Association's involvement was questioned.[32]

The Association had worked hard to get a City Planning Commission; should RPA now criticize this body? Should not RPA either support the Planning Commission or take a noncommittal attitude? Should RPA become involved in political action? Was it not enough to make public statements declaring its position on issues? Several directors raised these questions and expressed some misgivings over the measures that had been taken. These questions came from directors who tended to view RPA's function as being a nonpolitical maker of studies. To the extent that they perceived RPA's role as one of only very generalized, noncontroversial involvement, they were probably somewhat alarmed at the attack leveled against RPA by Moses. (Indeed, it may be that the harshness of Moses' attacks was calculated to discomfit those of RPA's supporters who viewed it as a nonpolitical research group.)

According to the minutes of the meeting, there was "full discussion." The board finally concluded:

It should be considered a proper part of the program of the Association, where the Board of Directors so authorize, not only to propose or endorse desirable projects; but to oppose such projects, or at least such major projects, as may seem undesirable and in its judgment against proper principles of city planning.[33]

Thus, the board sanctioned opposition as well as endorsement in the public policy field. Since RPA had publicly opposed projects it did not approve numerous times in the past, this statement was not breaking new ground. Also, it was not specific, probably deliberately, as to whether endorsement or opposition was to go beyond the making of statements. Thus, the nature of RPA's leadership role in influencing public policy was hardly clarified by this discussion. The matter was left in ambiguity, probably because general agreement on a more precise statement could not easily be reached.

The board went on to vote approval of McAneny's actions

and to record its continuing opposition to the Battery bridge proposal. The minutes do not record how the board divided in its vote on this motion of endorsement, although unanimous votes are often noted as such. This endorsement cannot clearly be taken as approval of the kind of leadership role envisioned by McAneny. He had, after all, executed a *fait accompli*. He had acted on a matter where RPA's position, based on the Regional Plan, was unmistakably clear. He and the Association had been subjected to public name-calling. Failure to endorse his actions under these circumstances would have been a rebuke to a dedicated and respected president.

In an organization valuing consensus highly, open questioning of the actions of the leaders, even by a fairly small minority, has its effect. Leaders may in the future go out of their way to avoid such incidents, even when confident of majority support. There is at least a hint that the criticism in this case had its effect. In making RPA's annual report for 1939, McAneny uncharacteristically glossed over this major political victory briefly and lightly.

The successful conclusion of this political foray thus does not appear to have strengthened RPA's commitment to a mildly active leadership role. Instead it pointed up the ambiguity of RPA's role and indicated that a segment of the board did not understand or accept McAneny's view of RPA's role. In the face of these conditions and of the increasing technical dominance of the organization, the survival of a vigorous leadership role in the region required able and aggressive internal leadership.

Summary

Much of the Regional Plan was executed or adopted during the 1930s. The public works proposals of the Plan, particularly those dealing with highways and river crossings, were largely carried out. The "success" of these aspects of the Plan may have been related to broader trends. Certainly much of this achievement is attributable to federal policies for public works spending. The federal stimulus also sparked the rapid proliferation of official planning bodies.

The conditions under which these developments took place tended to narrow RPA's focus and circumscribe its leadership role. The accomplishments of the 1930s were a result less of generation of substantial leadership and broad public support for planning than of the unique circumstances of the depression. The technicians on the staff dominated the promoters, public works engineering became the staff's major concern, and McAneny strained internal consensus by his involvement in the bridge controversy.

An ironic result of the successes of the 1930s was that the commitment to develop and exert broad regional leadership on planning questions was weakened by the very conditions that made these accomplishments possible. What would happen when the conditions of the 1930s had passed? How would RPA respond to the execution of most of the Regional Plan? RPA would soon have to develop new goals and to face the problems of defining and implementing a leadership role. RPA had not had to face these problems squarely in the 1930s.

CHAPTER IV

The Decline of Purpose

Disillusion and Dilemma

The final volume of the RPA's *From Plan to Reality* series, published in 1941, proudly noted the completion of or official commitment to more than half the recommendations of the 1929 Plan. Several years before, official planning agencies had been established in all the counties in the region and in many of the municipalities. RPA's goals, as stated in the Association's constitution, seemed to be largely achieved.

This apparent success raised questions of what RPA's subsequent program should be. McAneny's initial response to suggestions that RPA's mission was largely accomplished was to assert the importance of a "civic watchdog" role with respect to the region's new planning bodies:

Now that planning has been so generally recognized as a continuing responsibility of government and so from the nature of things is bound to take on a political hue, there is greater need than ever for the leadership, eternal vigilance, criticism, and the inspiration that can be afforded most generously and effectively only by this non-profit-making, non-partisan, non-political organization so truly representative of the aspirations of that great majority of citizens.[1]

It soon became apparent that McAneny's concerns were premature. He feared that these agencies would "take on a political hue." In fact, a majority of these planning bodies were largely dormant. A number of them disbanded entirely, not surviving the federal spending programs that had spurred their creation. Few had sufficient appropriations to support full-time staff services.

RPA tried to cope with some of these difficulties. In the late 1930s, it went beyond its earlier decision to provide technical assistance to local planning agencies on work relief proposals and decided to provide such assistance outside the context of public works proposals.[2] Such assistance would be provided by the RPA staff on a cost basis. Although no general announcement of this new policy was made, RPA began accepting the requests for assistance that periodically came to it. This program of technical assistance of local planning agencies was a major activity of the RPA staff for the next decade. Despite the stipulation that such work was to be done on a cost basis, rising costs of operations over time made this a deficit operation for the Association.

Lack of staff and budget did not exhaust the difficulties of the new planning bodies. Even the New York City Planning Commission proved to be a disappointment. Although well staffed and with an adequate budget, it spent its time largely on routine activities. RPA noted in 1941 that the most vital part of the Commission's statutory assignment, the preparation of a master plan of land uses, "came a cropper." The Commission had rejected the controversial master plan its staff had prepared, and the result "was to create a cloud of confusion around the subject of land use planning which it will take some time to dispel."[3]

There were more fundamental reasons for the more perceptive observers in RPA to be seriously concerned. Despite the achievements of the 1930s, it was obvious that the region was not becoming more "livable." An internal memorandum prepared by a top staff member in 1941 admitted that

Ownership of real estate in central areas seems to have become a liability instead of an asset. The quality of the region's population does not seem to have kept pace with its quantity. Blighted areas call for redevelopment while population swirls and migrates into raw land a few miles away. The region seems to be living on an allowance from the federal government.[4]

Why had the achievements of the Regional Plan and the official agencies not produced the anticipated results? It was apparent that some of RPA's assumptions about planning should be called into question. The final volume of the *From Plan to Reality* series ended with a peroration on much traditional planning doctrine:

The activity of local planning boards has, in general, not changed greatly in character in recent years, when the functions of government as a whole were changing and expanding a great deal. The planning idea was pioneered in an era of growth; its original philosophy was the orderly guidance of growth. . . . In the past ten years, . . . only a few planning boards have seen the need to rethink their function, and to become diagnosticians coordinating the host of new remedial government functions which seek to promote industrial stability, alleviate social insecurity, and exterminate urban blight. Many planning agencies have stayed within the older boundaries of planning land use and physical improvements, and have lapsed into inactivity on the grounds that since no funds were available to finance physical improvements, there was nothing for planning boards to do.

In summation, a review of accomplishments or lack of them in local planning in the Region points to the vital need of a functioning staff, concerning itself with the total problem of the municipality and the coordination of the work of each executive branch. The early philosophy of planning organization, function, and operating methods has come into serious question. That philosophy conceived the planning agency as concerned almost exclusively with land use and major physical improvements, maintaining a somewhat distrustful, watchdog attitude toward elected officials, and imparting wisdom from a special abode detached from the everyday administration of political offices.

Experience indicates that boards operating on this philosophy have gone to sleep. Successful planning has been characterized by closer contact with the governing body and operating officials, with greater emphasis on the coordinating role; by the provision of expert, full-time personnel; and by a broader conception of the planning function corresponding to the broadened functions of government.[5]

Both the narrowly physical conception of planning and the notion of the "independent" planning commission detached from the executive are drawn into question. Planning is viewed here as a staff function of the executive branch, with a scope of concerns as broad as the functions of government.

This criticism did not necessarily represent a shift of emphasis or commitment on the part of RPA; a change of commitment requires not only explicit definition but also institutionalization within the organization. This statement is significant, however, in pointing up the early disillusionment with RPA's achievements.

RPA faced serious problems. The New Deal period had "used up" most of the relevant public works proposals of the Regional Plan, so that the Association's platform steadily diminished. Furthermore, as federal public works spending declined and as World War II brought a substantial moratorium on many kinds of public works and planning developments, RPA tended to lose its audience—the primary attention of all levels of government was usually directed elsewhere. In sum, RPA, in the early 1940s, saw both its platform and its audience vanishing. Its "success" of the 1930s proved to be more limited than had been expected. RPA's survival seemed to call for the development of new programs, possibly even alteration of basic commitments.

FINANCIAL PROBLEMS

An additional component of the crisis confronting RPA was a steadily declining financial status. After 1936, RPA's income steadily diminished, reaching an all-time low in 1943.[6] The Russell Sage Foundation, in agreeing to continue its support of RPA, had stipulated that the amount of its annual grants would taper off, with the Association presumably recruiting more independent sources of support. Consequently, the annual grant from Russell Sage declined from a high of $50,500 in 1933 to $20,000 in 1941 and to $15,000 in 1947. Much of this reduction was replaced by nonrecurring grants from other foundations, notably the Carnegie Corporation and the Spelman Fund, rather than by regular recurring contributions of members and subscribers. This postponed rather than solved the financial problem. Even with this additional support, RPA was forced to borrow money in 1937 and 1938.

The steady decline in corporate contributions after 1937 is almost certainly related to the decline in a sense of purpose that occurred as disillusion followed achievement. The contributors who abandoned RPA in this period had been recruited during the earlier years of the depression and had stayed with RPA during the years of its most substantial achievements. It is unlikely that poor economic conditions formed a major reason for this decline. This seems all the more unlikely, since the decline continued through the war years, when substantial economic recovery took place.

During the first half of the 1940s, only a hard core of six firms contributed $500 or more annually to RPA.[7] These probably represent the irreducible core of the most interested and most committed of RPA's corporate constituency. The six firms were the Consolidated Edison Company, the Metropolitan Life Insurance Company, the Bowery Savings Bank, the New York Telephone Company, the New Jersey Bell Telephone Company, and the Hackensack Water Company. In this period RPA had almost literally no one else, and the aggregate contribution of these firms amounted to no great sum.

A further complication was the retirement of McAneny as president of the Association in 1940. Although he remained active in the Association for some years, he gave up the fund-raising responsibilities that he had largely shouldered by himself. A year later, RPA's new executive vice-president stated that RPA had survived financially "only because of some magic of Mr. McAneny." [8]

Immediate financial crisis was averted in 1940, when the Association secured a gift of $100,000 from an anonymous donor, who set no conditions or restrictions on its use. The directors decided to use this as part of the regular operating budget, gaining at least a temporary respite from financial crisis. However, new sources of support would eventually have to be developed.

ALTERNATIVES

All these factors—the Regional Plan being largely used up, the failures of many of the planning agencies, disappointment in regional development trends, and declining financial support—combined to place RPA at a point of critical decision. It could go out of business altogether; it could continue to maintain a small technical staff, turn out research reports, and forsake a more active role; or it could devise a new set of program goals to succeed the Regional Plan, renew its commitment to organize regional leadership, and become again an active influence on regional development.

Although some RPA leaders are reported to have viewed it as a more broadly based continuation of the Committee on the Regional Plan, with a specific job to do, there is no indication of serious consideration of disbanding at this time. A pure research role, providing financial support could be obtained, was a natural possibility. RPA could continue to aid local planning bodies, make fact-finding studies, and propagate the principles of good planning. This would seriously subordinate any commitment to regional leadership. Lacking a comprehensive program comparable to the Regional Plan, RPA was without a clear focus for a leadership role. RPA could keep alive its regional leadership role only by developing a new set of integrated program goals into which an active leadership commitment could be integrated.

New Leadership

Important changes in organizational role are often accompanied by significant personnel changes. During the period of 1940–42, RPA experienced a reshuffling of staff personnel in an effort to design new goals.

McAneny, long a source of strong leadership and great vitality, retired as president in 1940. Frederick C. Horner, an engineer, later to become assistant to the president for direction of field operations of General Motors Corporation, agreed to serve a short term as president. Because of duties with federal agencies after the outbreak of World War II, Horner resigned in 1942 and was succeeded by Paul Windels, an attorney with a substantial background in public affairs.[9]

The most important change came at the staff level. Leaders of the board were convinced that an able nontechnician might more effectively coordinate the technical and promotional staffs. Consequently, the post of executive vice-president was created in 1940, and C. McKim Norton, already a director of the Association, was chosen to fill it. Harold Lewis, a civil engineer who had headed the staff since 1938, remained with the title of chief engineer and planning officer.

Norton, the son of Charles Dyer Norton, was a lawyer. Before coming to RPA, he had served as counsel to the National Resources Planning Board, headed by Delano. Reared in the Norton-Delano tradition of civic leadership, he represented continuity with the organization's past, was readily acceptable to all participants, and was skilled in the arts of reconciling differences. He was well suited to be a liaison between the directors and the technical staff as well as between the divergent wings of the staff.

Norton came to his new position convinced of the urgent need for some redirection of RPA's program. Soon after assuming his new duties, he prepared a memorandum for Horner, in which he sketched his ideas for the Association's future. In it, he noted the division between engineering and promotional staffs:

The two groups never merged. . . . Judging from past budgets, the engineering staff dominated this organization. The publications of the Association emphasized physical plans, especially those dealing with highways and transportation problems. The promotional staff concentrated on stimulating the organization of local planning by citizen planning boards, most of which are today dormant.[10]

Norton granted that there had been notable successes: "The decade of the 1930's was peculiarly susceptible to the accomplishment of the physical factors of the Regional Plan by the engineering approach." These gains had come at a price, however: "In the process the Association has lost touch with its membership and with the public." He concluded: "Something more than a list of desirable public works is needed by the region. . . . Would the objectives of the Regional Plan really be realized if such works were constructed tomorrow?"[11]

Norton made six general recommendations for the Association:

1. Reduce the permanent engineering staff to a minimum required to keep the plan map physically up to date.

2. Make more special reports on vital topics, such as the current traffic and parking survey, the economic trends survey, a bus terminal survey, a new study of blighted areas and how to reconstruct them under new laws, a thorough study of the effect of air travel on the region and its airports, an analysis of federal spending in the region, and a study of the efficiency of port facilities.

3. Set up a reference service and library so as to make the Association the clearing house of all research on the region, wherever undertaken.

4. Study regional trends and establish a series of indices so that the Association can advise as to where the region seems to be going both within itself and as compared with other metropolitan areas.

5. Revise "fieldwork" by change of staff so as to present a more practical approach in stimulating planning throughout the region.

6. Gradually revise the board of directors.[12]

Norton's greatest interest was strengthening and broadening RPA's research operations beyond the narrow engineering ap-

proach that had prevailed in the 1930s. His intentions with respect to RPA's leadership functions were less specific, although
a strengthening of this role was envisioned.

The board of directors authorized Norton to carry out the
staff changes suggested in his memorandum. The new emphasis
Norton sought was reflected in some key shifts of personnel.
In January, 1942, Lewis was replaced by Frederick P. Clark,
the planning director of the New Hampshire State Planning
and Development Commission. Clark had been trained as an
architect, but his entire career had been spent in planning.
He assumed the title of planning director.

At the same time, the position of field secretary was eliminated. The Association was now abandoning active missionary
work on behalf of the neighborhood unit, and the promotion
of planning that had gone on before was now curtailed.

The new staff leadership and most of the board were now
in general agreement that the 1929 Regional Plan was no
longer an adequate base for the Association's program. They
were less certain as to what new goals should be sought. The
first statement of purpose submitted to the board by the new
planning director stated three principal program goals:

> The current program of the RPA should be directed to three prin-
> cipal ends: (1) assisting with such studies and plans as will facilitate
> the war effort, and (2) preparation of plans for the post-war period,
> and (3) continued promotion of the cause of official planning.[13]

Several board members expressed uneasiness about the gen-
erality of these objectives, stating that more specific goals
should be elaborated. Although general, this statement is the
first declaration of purpose to omit reference to the Regional
Plan of 1929. It was a tacit acknowledgment of the need to
move on to new goals and policies.

The Economic Survey of the Region

The response of the staff to the demand for more specific
objectives was not long in coming. Norton was highly inter-

ested in having RPA study regional economic trends. He had noted earlier that one of the objectives of the 1929 Plan had been to promote the economic efficiency of the region. The first of the survey volumes that preceded the Plan was an economic survey of the region, and economic feasibility was one of the criteria used in some of the choices embodied in the Regional Plan. When the Plan was presented to the public in 1929, one of its most notable advances over the earlier emphasis on "city beautiful" planning was said to be the greater attention to social and economic considerations.

Norton strongly believed that the intentions of the founders and the broad purposes of the Regional Plan had been obscured in the stress on public works engineering during the 1930s. He also felt that an economic studies program would give RPA a more tangible appeal and help in securing additional corporate support. Such a program, he felt, should be accompanied by a broadening of the board of directors to make it a more effective leadership force.

Such a program was recommended by the staff in November, 1942. It provided for an economic survey of the region, to be used as a basis for postwar planning. The proposal cited the apparent economic decline of the region: 'The New York Metropolitan Region . . . is in danger of facing community bankruptcy in the post-war world." Public works alone were inadequate:"These structures are of value only if they are used by a busy population engaged in productive enterprise." [14] Further, the business community was chastened for not meeting its civic responsibilities:

Since 1929, the men who built twentieth century New York have stood on the sidelines watching government wrestle with a decade of depression. . . . While private business stood on the sidelines and watched . . . evidences of economic decay, the structure of the region's cities grew old and obsolete. . . .

The New York Metropolitan Area is not a small town where one leading citizen can spark the whole community. The area is, indeed, so vast and complex that its individual citizens have all but given up understanding its problems. Yet a group of men with power to translate their ideas into action, organized properly into working units and inspiring the cooperation of all private and public agencies equipped to assist them, could act effectively now to mobilize the forces of the New York Metropolitan Area to meet the challenge of a changing world. . . . It is essential that the officers, the Board of Directors and the staff undertake to secure active participation in the Association's program by representative citizens who have a stake in the several fields of development encompassed in the Association's overall program.[15]

Here, then, were the changes the staff was seeking: abandonment of narrow physical planning, study of economic trends, and a broadening of the board to include more "representative citizens" with important regional interests. The organization of regional leadership was seen as an integral element of the proposed program.

The executive committee of the board directed Paul Windels, who had just become RPA's president, and ex-president George McAneny to revise the staff proposal. Windels and McAneny, sensing that the need for broad innovation might not be self-evident to some board members, took a more conservative approach, calculated to preserve consensus and secure the most immediate recommendation of the staff. They condensed the six-page document to a less outspoken two pages, from which strong suggestions of crisis were absent and which omitted references to the civic failures of the business community and to changing the board of directors. The new emphasis on economics was spelled out more explicitly, and the continuity of this proposal with RPA's past was noted:

The proposed program will seek answers to three basic questions which vitally affect the future of the New York region. First, what will be the effect of changing world economic conditions and means of transportation on the Port of New York? Second, recognizing increasing competition from other metropolitan areas of the United States for the location of commercial and industrial establishments, what types of business and industry can the New York region expect to retain and what new types can it logically expect to attract? Third, what internal problems of the New York Region must be solved in order to maintain the Region on an effective competitive basis and make it more efficient and liveable in the light of answers to the above stated questions? . . . This program is one of new emphasis rather than a new departure.[16]

The instincts of McAneny and Windels proved to be correct. The board of directors endorsed the undertaking of the proposed economic studies, but the discussion of the matter suggests that this endorsement was less a firm commitment to a new program than a cautious, guarded probing of possible new lines of activity.

Some members of the board expressed concern about the relation of economic studies to RPA's traditional functions. The basis on which many accepted the proposal was its presumed relationship to physical planning: "There was general agreement that . . . this survey is needed in order to reappraise the physical Regional Plan proposals." [17]

Another qualification raised in the discussion was whether the ultimate aim of this research would be enhancement of economic competitiveness for its own sake or enhancement of the general quality of life in the region. It was argued that the broad justification for all RPA's activity was improving the attractiveness of the region as a place to live, work, and bring up families. RPA should be something more than a chamber of commerce with a strong research arm. Those who voiced these concerns strongly felt that the economic survey should be clearly related to broader social concerns.

Various elements in the Association continued to voice second thoughts about this program while it was in progress. These most often centered on the relevance of these studies to physical planning. Windels, addressing the Association's annual meeting in 1944, stated that, with the economic studies approaching completion, the preponderance of staff time would again be devoted "to problems concerned with the physical development of the region." [18]

These doubts suggest the continuing strength of the several inducements to involvement in RPA indicated in Chapter II.

For many directors the new studies had to be shown to be related significantly to physical planning; for others RPA was seen as a philanthropic organization with a broad concern for "livability." The "cash-value" significance of this program was not enough, by itself, to justify it to an apparently substantial segment of the board. Despite these reservations, the directors approved the proposal. An economist was added to the staff on an *ad hoc* basis and was given the title director of economic studies. The studies, oriented toward postwar trends, were hopefully to serve the purposes the Regional Plan had served earlier and to provide a set of regional development policies for RPA to promote.

Wartime Uncertainties

The war years were dismal ones for state and local governments generally. RPA, consequently, lost a substantial part of the audience it had in the 1930s. RPA also lacked a concrete program, as the most marketable proposals of the Regional Plan had been adopted. The economic survey was a tentative probing and was directed to postwar problems. In these circumstances, it is not surprising that RPA's attitude was one of considerable caution, uncertainty, and reluctance to venture beyond customary ways of behaving.

The RPA staff continued to make studies. Several studies of specific problems were undertaken, and the staff engaged in a variety of technical planning studies, in preparation of land use and other physical maps, and in other planning research. Norton, soon after becoming executive vice-president of RPA, developed a scheme of research organization calculated to provide more effective channels of communication with official agencies. The Association undertook a study of traffic problems and parking needs for New York City in 1940 and invited staff members from relevant city agencies and other civic organizations to participate in the study and in the drafting of recommendations based on the study.[19] This was the first of numerous ventures where RPA sought to involve staff members from official agencies in RPA studies. This organizational pattern has been one means of recruiting some support, at least at the staff level, within some of the agencies that possess authority to carry out the recommendations.

Norton and Clark were both in military service from 1943 to 1945, so that the staff lacked guidance from its permanent leaders in those years. One of the staff engineers assumed temporary direction of the staff during those years.

THE STUYVESANT TOWN PROJECT

When faced with novel or controversial situations, the Association in this period tended to react very guardedly and did not seek to become actively involved in public issues. This is well illustrated by one of the most serious controversies within the RPA board, precipitated by the issue of urban renewal in 1943.[20]

The State of New York enacted legislation providing public subsidies for private developers interested in some types of urban renewal projects. Under this legislation, the Metropolitan Life Insurance Company sought to construct a middle-income housing development, which ultimately became Stuyvesant Town. When hearings were held before the City Planning Commission, Paul Windels appeared and presented a statement approved by the RPA board supporting the project. The statement was confined to a general recognition of the need for urban redevelopment and sound renewal and redevelopment policies. The Stuyvesant Town proposal was lauded as a hopeful development but was not commented on in any detail.

Other interested organizations opposed the project and tried to persuade RPA to reexamine its position. It was argued that the project would violate several important planning standards that RPA had usually championed, including density, relation to community facilities and services, and other matters. RPA was urged to join with several other civic organizations in a legal action to reverse the approval given by the City Planning Commission.

These appeals found some support on the RPA board. Some directors noted that the density of the project, school location, and the closing of public ways through the project were all objectionable. Others had doubts about the use of public funds for housing developments of this kind. Windels defended the project, stating that it was "the most hopeful thing that has happened in the rebuilding of the City in many a year."

RPA's problem was complicated by the fact that substantial governmental roles in urban renewal and redevelopment were largely unknown in the days when the Regional Plan was developed. RPA had no clear inherited doctrine on questions like this and lacked a new set of program goals from which a clear position might be derived.

Faced by a serious difference of opinion on the Board, RPA declined either to reaffirm or to reverse its previous position. A statement of RPA's general policy concerning public issues was adopted: "RPA policy is to limit itself to statements of basic principles of sound redevelopment and refrain from getting into details of particular plans." This was a very narrow interpretation of RPA's leadership function and an obvious retreat from the role which McAneny had urged earlier. Under the prevailing conditions of change and uncertainty, however, and without a definite program, this position was probably inevitable. Although RPA has given vigorous support to urban renewal in later years, this limited statement was probably the most that could be agreed on by a divided board facing this question for the first time.

THE REGIONAL AIRPORT PLAN

The most important involvement of RPA in public policy in the 1940s occurred in the preparation, jointly with the Port of New York Authority, of the Regional Airport Plan, published in 1946.[21]

New York's Mayor La Guardia, who had earlier spear-headed the construction of La Guardia Airport, was pressing for the construction of a much larger, more modern facility at Idlewild, Queens. The airport recommendations of the 1929 Regional Plan were rapidly becoming dated, and RPA's leaders wanted to salvage some of these and to influence some of the upcoming airport decisions before the Plan proposals became completely obsolete.

Accordingly, C. McKim Norton, just before entering the service, approached William A. Burden, Assistant Secretary of Commerce, whose jurisdiction included the Civil Aeronautics Administration. Norton wanted federal backing for a revision of the airport proposals of the 1929 Plan, recalling the happy relations between RPA and the federal public works agencies in the 1930s. Kaufman, in his account of the controversy over the administration of the New York airports, states:

The timing of the inquiry was fortunate, for Burden was looking for a group to prepare a Regional Airport Plan for the New York area to fit into the National Airport Plan being compiled by the C.A.A. The C.A.A., in turn, needed the material to provide a basis for a request for funds from Congress for the construction and improvement of airports over the entire nation, which ultimately resulted in the Federal Airport Act of 1946.[22]

RPA invited representatives of the Port Authority to a meeting addressed by Burden to discuss the development of such a plan. The Port Authority had staff resources that would be valuable for the study, and the Authority's interstate charter made it a logical body for the administration and coordination of a regional system of airports. The Airport Plan was organized as a joint undertaking of RPA and the Port Authority, strengthening already friendly ties between them.

The Airport Plan, using the 1929 Plan as a point of departure, urged "the fullest development of four major airports, eight supplementary major airports, 18 secondary airports, 51 local airports, and 36 seaplane bases over the length and breadth of the region." [23]

The Plan made no novel suggestions for sites for major airports, since the Idlewild site had already been chosen by the city. The execution of the Plan, however, would require legal and financial powers beyond those of the city. The Plan therefore proposed a new tri-state regional agency.

RPA gained a symbolic victory of some importance when the Plan was officially adopted by the Civil Aeronautics Administration in 1946—the first time that a regionwide plan had been adopted by a single governmental agency that had jurisdiction over the entire metropolitan area.

The question remained of who would manage the region's airport system. The Port Authority had recently been requested to take over management of the Newark Airport, and the contest in New York City was between the City Airport Authority, a brainchild of Robert Moses, and the Port Authority. RPA, having gone on record in favor of a tri-state agency, decided, predictably, that the regional status of the Port Authority rendered it preferable to a city authority (especially one that Moses would probably dominate). RPA may have been co-opted by the Port Authority in this instance, but there is no indication that RPA would have decided differently had it been operating alone. RPA gained in prestige and reputation, even though its role in influencing the ultimate decision by the city seems to have been less than crucial.

Why was the airport issue able to engage the energies of RPA where other issues largely failed to do so? This was one of the areas where the proposals of the 1929 Regional Plan had not been largely carried out. Although many of the airport proposals of the 1929 Plan were dated in detail, the general framework of these recommendations was not yet irrelevant. In short, this was a matter clearly within RPA's customary focus of interest and one where RPA's initial program still contained relevant material. Consequently, although RPA may not have been a decisive factor in the decisions that were made, RPA was not reluctant to become actively involved. The airport issue, then, is the major exception to the general pattern of cautious restraint and noninvolvement that generally prevailed in these uncertain years.

Search for a Platform and an Audience

The main hope for developing a new postwar program had centered on the economic study that Norton had actively promoted. However, this study did not yield the anticipated results. A variety of reasons have been suggested for this failure. Some staff members reported that the study assumed the probability of a postwar depression and made other assumptions that were not borne out. It is also possible that, after the departure of the economists from the staff, the engineers and planners did not know exactly what to do with the studies. For whatever reasons, the hopes anticipated at the beginning of this project failed to be realized.

Recognizing the inability of the Association to generate new goals from the recently completed economic survey, Norton and Clark, on returning to RPA in 1945, prepared a memorandum for the directors, calling for "broad revision of the Regional Plan itself as regards not only physical improvements but also meeting the basic issues of land use and density of population." [24]

Invoking the Regional Plan may have had some symbolic value, but the Plan was rapidly becoming irrelevant to the actual pattern of postwar development. It had been apparent since the late 1930s that the region was not developing in the basic pattern envisioned by the 1929 Plan. The makers of the Plan, seeking some relief of the congestion in the central-city areas, envisioned a controlled pattern of suburban development, with clusterings of suburban communities around major transportation arteries. They foresaw a limited decentralization taking place, with a handful of clusters of suburban development, their limits prescribed largely by the location of transportation facilities.

The prime flaw in this picture was a gross underestimation of the automobile. The region's decision-makers committed themselves increasingly to the rubber tire. Highway construction soon outstripped the projections of the Regional Plan, while the expansion of rail lines and the creation of suburban rapid transit arrangements lagged more than any other feature of the Plan. The rapid development of the region's highways and the overwhelming popular preference for automotive transportation helped significantly to create a region far more decentralized, with far more uncontrolled urban sprawl, than the makers of the Regional Plan had imagined. Between 1925 and 1940 the region's population increased 26 percent; its built-up area increased 56 percent. Over the same fifteen-year period, there was a net population decline of almost 700,000 in Manhattan, Brooklyn, Jersey City, and Newark.[25]

These trends were evident before the war. After the war, they proceeded rapidly. In 1948, the Association stated that:

Today it takes almost as much land to house less than 14,000,000 people as the original Committee on the Regional Plan of New York and Its Environs thought would be adequate for 21,000,000 people.[26]

Other developments unforseen by the Regional Plan were summarized later by Windels:

Governmental support for housing has had a tremendous and unforeseen impact. Improving economic conditions made it possible for more people to live in the suburbs than had been anticipated. This, in turn, tended to speed up the process of obsolescence in the older areas, which, again in turn, compelled a broadening of the area of governmental responsibility and interest until we have finally arrived at the concept of wholesale neighborhood rebuilding by federal funds.[27]

With this pattern of scatteration and urban sprawl proceeding apace, the Regional Plan was every day less relevant as a framework for a meaningful RPA program, no matter what revisions might be made.

The Association's position was apparent to the staff and to the directors. Of the many declarations of purpose adopted at various times by the RPA Board, none is more modest than the one officially approved on December 20, 1945:

The work of the Association is composed of two principal activities: first, the basic research and planning for the Region's growth and development, and second, assistance in meeting the specific planning problems that arise from day to day.[28]

Promotional activity, omitted from this statement, was not totally discontinued but continued to decline. In submitting a proposed program for 1950, the staff stated: "The program contemplated is primarily one of research activity, reducing the volume of public appearances and activity to hearings and appearances of major importance." [29]

RPA was drifting into an increasing emphasis on research and technical studies. This was not a deliberate choice but a result of the failure to develop a definite set of regional development policies. The Association's leadership role would decline also; such a role could not be exercised without commitment to definite policy positions. That RPA was becoming increasingly oriented to technology and declining as a source of regional leadership was perceived by some of the interested elements of the regional community. The New York *Herald Tribune* noted editorially that

One of [RPA's] main activities should be to knit up the ravelings of controversy and help give all of us . . . a better view of the city we want. . . . But . . . the association has become preoccupied with questions of planning technique and methods to such an extent that the very language of the planners now makes the eye glaze with incomprehension and indifference. Public interest in what should be a broad democratic process is becoming stultified. . . . The Regional Plan Association should assume the leadership that is indispensable if public thinking is to be cohesive and public action decisive.[30]

THE SEARCH CONTINUES

RPA's leaders, especially Windels and Norton, were not narrow-minded technicians. They tried hard to respond to this challenge to set new goals and become once again a center of regional leadership. They engaged in a wide-ranging search for new ideas, and Windels' speeches in the late 1940s contained numerous new lines of thought

Addressing a National Citizens Conference on Planning in Newark in 1948, Windels advocated "that we deliberately design and create entirely new and distinctive self-sufficient communities for the purpose of accomodating a substantial part of our regional growth." [31] Two years later, in a speech before the American Institute of Architects, Windels called for co-operative action by the states to create Metropolitan District Commissions and to form New Town Development Corporations.[32]

Windels' search was for an audience as well as for a platform. He repeatedly called on the states to take more responsibility in metropolitan planning. In his 1950 speech before the American Institute of Architects, he called for a federal urban policy:

Entirely aside from military defense, few people realize how important a factor the Federal Government has become in the development of the nation's cities. For the past twenty years it has exercised a powerful influence upon the form and character of city growth. It, therefore, has a grave and direct responsibility for the cumulative effects of its policies.[33]

None of these suggestions produced a significant positive response at the time. Some RPA directors were reportedly somewhat alarmed at the scope of some of Windels' proposals. In the meantime, RPA had to be provided with a reason for going beyond research work if the leadership commitment was to be kept alive. Windels found a new way of stating a *raison d'être* for RPA:

When we consider that this metropolitan area includes more than 500 autonomous units of government, each with some authority to make and enforce development policies, the need of a coordinating influence is at once apparent. The Regional Plan Association is the only agency—public or private—which presently exists for this purpose. It is the reason for its existence.[34]

To implement this coordinating role, Windels called a meeting of representatives of the seven official county planning boards in the region and of the New York City Planning Commission. This group met on January 11, 1950, and formed the Metropolitan Council of Planning Agencies, which subsequently met periodically under RPA auspices.[35]

Windels' emphasis on coordination was not a new doctrine; the very existence of the Regional Plan was supposed to have facilitated coordination. As a general goal, coordination, by itself, begs important questions. Into what kind of overall policy framework and schedule of priorities will the efforts of various governmental units be coordinated? Or will the coordinating process more or less automatically evolve a policy framework? Coordination as RPA's basic goal may be another manifestation of the increasingly technical emphasis within the Association.

After searching for new goals for some time, RPA decided in 1949 to apply to several foundations to see if funds could be secured for another regional plan. A proposal was developed which called for a plan, generally along the lines of the 1929 Plan, to be made over a three-year period at a cost of approximately $1.5 million.[36] After the plan was made, it could then "be translated effectively to reality through similar methods so successfully developed and carried out for the Regional Plan of 1929." [37] Foundation support could not be secured, however; RPA apparently was not going to be able to develop the urgently needed new program without some broad rethinking of its basic commitments and its organizational role.

INTERNAL PROBLEMS

RPA faced a continuing financial crisis as well as a program crisis. Corporate support dwindled to approximately $10,000 per year during the dismal years of 1942–45 (Table 3). The final Russell Sage grant was to be made in 1948.

TABLE 3

REGIONAL PLAN ASSOCIATION INCOME, 1929–50

Year *	Membership Dues †	Corporate Subscriptions †	Foundations, Special Studies, and Miscellaneous	Total
1929	$10,600		$25,000	$ 35,600
1930	53,500		35,000	88,500
1931	48,000		33,000	81,000
1932	23,900		80,300	104,200
1933	25,500		57,450	82,950
1934	24,900		48,800	73,700
1935	23,400		50,600	74,000
1936	22,500		64,600	87,100
1937	30,700		49,300	80,000
1938	22,900		30,000	52,900
1939	21,800		32,000	53,800
1940	$5,000	$16,000	35,700	56,700
1941	5,372	17,150	26,747	49,269
1942	5,545	10,250	29,398	45,193
1943	4,413	10,000	29,724	44,137
1944	4,660	10,300	24,980	39,940
1945	4,780	10,801	21,373	36,954
1946	8,504 ‡	15,500	38,656	62,660
1947	3,274	35,304	27,966	66,544
1948	3,380	38,097	48,312	89,789
1949	3,735	40,958	9,909	54,602
1950	3,572	39,198	6,610	49,380

* Data for later years appended to Chapter VII.
† RPA records do not distinguish membership dues and corporate subscriptions prior to 1940.
‡ Memberships or corporate subscriptions under $500.

Key board members tried to raise funds from their business colleagues. This brought a significant increase in income but did not represent much broadening of RPA's financial base. Some old contributors increased their gifts, and the new ones generally were the same kinds of businesses as those already supporting RPA. For example, Earl Schwulst, president of the Bowery Savings Bank, intensively canvassed other savings bank presidents; several utility executives on the board solicited other utility executives. Major new contributors recruited in the immediate postwar period included the Brooklyn Union Gas Company, the Long Island Lighting Company, Central Hudson Gas and Electric, the Long Island and New Haven Railroads, and several savings banks.[38] By 1950, RPA had nineteen contributors whose annual contribution was $500 or more. They include seven utilities, six savings banks, three insurance companies, one commercial bank, one department store, and one industrial concern.

Although contributions increased, this increase was not enough to prevent a severe shock when the final Russell Sage grant was spent. This final grant, a sum of $36,000, was made in 1948. In 1949, a deficit of $17,000 was incurred and was covered by the special fund set up by the large anonymous gift in 1940, but this payment of the deficit left only $5,000 in this fund. With a deficit for the following year a certainty, a genuine crisis had arrived.

RPA's response was a rigorous belt-tightening. An engineer, the public relations director, and a part-time secretary were released and not replaced, a draftsman who was leaving the organization was not replaced, and Norton volunteered to serve for one year without pay, an offer the directors reluctantly had to accept. Membership dues were doubled (from $5 to $10), and technical services for local planning bodies were eliminated (this had usually been a deficit operation). Despite all these measures, a small deficit, slightly over $1,000, was incurred the following year.

Over a period of more than a decade, RPA searched for a new platform and a new audience. Not clearly finding either, it was moving inadvertently toward a technical and research role which would not require strong commitment to the exercise of a leadership role. RPA's leadership functions were languishing largely because of failure to evolve a concrete program of regional goals comparable to the 1929 Plan.

Whether RPA's policy development and leadership functions could be resurrected was problematic. Unless its financial condition could be improved, its survival for any purpose was in jeopardy.

CHAPTER V

The Rehabilitation
of Purpose: I

The problem faced by the RPA is one that has confronted many groups at critical stages in their development. When a group's initial goals are achieved or rendered irrelevant, where does the group turn? Does it generate new goals, or does it retreat to a position of valuing what had originally been a means now as an end in itself? Or does it go out of business? Many organizations committed to definite limited goals have found themselves in this kind of dilemma.

Responses to such a crisis vary. A militant labor union, for example, accustomed to relying on appeals of class antagonism and mass mobilization of workers, may attain its initial goals of recognition. It may then turn to more conservative goals and techniques that will stabilize relations with management and maintain a responsible organization. Selznick had noted a widespread turnover of personnel in the United Automobile Workers as it underwent a basic shift of emphasis from militance to more moderate bargaining techniques.[1]

In the same way, the National Foundation for Infantile Paralysis saw its goals largely accomplished with the development and mass distribution of vaccines to prevent polio. Instead of folding its tents, it responded by developing new goals and commitments.[2]

The Ford Motor Company is cited by Selznick as an illustration of this problem in industry. Reluctantly, over a period of some years, and at a substantial cost, Ford shifted its basic commitment from efficient production exclusively to placing advertising and public relations at least on a par with production.[3]

This condition, which Blau and Scott call "succession of goals" (initial achievements being succeeded by a new set of objectives),[4] presents special problems of internal leadership to civic groups. While broad agreement on original goals may have been possible, consensus on new commitments may be difficult to achieve. Truman has called attention to the role of overlapping memberships in complicating the task of internal management of consensus.[5] Discussing civic organizations in Chicago, Banfield has noted that, even under the best of circumstances, civic groups are likely to be strongly inhibited by internal conflict and preoccupation with organizational maintenance.[6]

Blau and Scott stress the relation of the group to its environment in the determination of whether or not a succession of goals takes place.[7] Where the environment is unpromising or hostile, innovation is less likely and withdrawal more probable. The greater the adversity of the environment, the greater the task of internal leadership in promoting innovation.

RPA had operated in a highly discouraging environment during the 1940s. In the 1950s, however, its environment began to change. Signs of increasing concern with regional problems and planning began to be manifested.

RPA itself had, in 1950, successfully sired the Metropolitan Council of Planning Agencies, a periodic gathering of representatives of the region's official planning bodies. In New York City increasing interest was shown in comprehensive rezoning, the transportation problems of the region were becoming increasingly urgent, and in 1954 the states of New York and New Jersey created a Metropolitan Rapid Transit Commission to study trans-Hudson transportation. The utilities, the public authorities, and other groups felt an increasing need for more adequate regional economic and demographic data. In 1956 Mayor Wagner called a conference of the elected chief executives of the counties and municipalities of the region, resulting in the formation of the Metropolitan Regional Council as a continuing voluntary unofficial vehicle for cooperation and collaboration among the region's political leaders.

Indeed, all over the United States there was growing awareness of metropolitan problems. Increasing population, rapid and uncontrolled growth, problems of transportation, recreation, industrial location, urban redevelopment, and many others were creating crises that could not be ignored by either public or business decision-makers. The concerns of planners were being moved from the status of advanced concerns of urban esthetics to that of serious policy questions. Suggestions for a federal cabinet-level Department of Urban Affairs began to be heard. Forces were at work that could help give RPA a new lease on life.

Another Proposal for Economic Studies

Facing an environment that was beginning to look promising, RPA acquired new leadership in 1952. Paul Windels was succeeded as president by Harold Osborne, who had just retired as chief engineer of the American Telephone and Telegraph Company. At about the same time, Henry Fagin replaced Frederick Clark as planning director. Like Clark, Fagin was trained in architecture and came to RPA with substantial experience as a professional planner. Both Osborne and Fagin were exceptionally able men, and, along with Norton, rapidly initiated innovations.

RPA's staff was the smallest since the depression. Although it was obvious that fundamental changes were taking place in the region, RPA, given the limitations of its staff and budget, could do no more than skim the surface of emerging development trends in its research. An upgrading of RPA's research efforts appeared to be the first order of business.

Late in 1952 the Long Island Lighting Company approached

RPA with a request for population projections for Nassau and Suffolk Counties in order to improve the company's load-forecasting procedures.[8] RPA was not able to produce reliable data on which such projections could be based. This was a serious problem; many utility companies have always been firm supporters of RPA, and one incentive for such support has been the value of RPA research in just such matters as this.

Fagin believed that a physical survey estimating probable density patterns was not enough; no physical survey could predict the timing of probable population growth. The Long Island counties would grow mainly by immigration, and a particularly important aspect of a calculation of immigration was a study of employment trends in the major divisions of business and industry and the distribution of such employment throughout the region. These factors, as well as industrial development generally, could be studied meaningfully only on a regional basis. Fagin believed, in short, that a comprehensive economic survey of the region was an indispensable requisite for carrying out the research and information service valued by key supporters.

Fagin outlined his ideas for a revised method of population forecasting based on a regional survey of industrial location and employment trends to several technicians from Long Island Lighting and Consolidated Edison.[9] All expressed keen interest, and one suggested that RPA call together representatives of all the major utilities for suggestions and assistance in carrying out such a project.

Shortly thereafter, RPA organized a "forecasting committee" composed of RPA staff and technicians from twelve of the region's major utilities. This group met six times over the next few months and formulated an outline of a study of regional economic trends. Consultants from Columbia University and Massachusetts Institute of Technology were retained to assess the research design and to provide time and cost estimates.

Fagin was attempting to turn RPA's research efforts once

more toward economic analysis and to upgrade RPA's service functions for its supporters. What he was proposing, however, differed in several respects from the studies of the 1940s. Fagin's proposal involved a larger scale of operation and more sophisticated techniques of inquiry. The studies of the 1940s were initiated by leaders of the RPA staff. For the designing of this project Fagin drew in a number of staff personnel from businesses that could be expected to utilize the resulting research, thus assuring maximum relevance to the needs of RPA's constituency. Three major objectives of the project were cited:

Objectives of project. (1) To discover the principal forces that determine where within a metropolitan region the key economic activities tend to locate.

(2) To understand what long-run effect these locational forces will have on the distribution of economic activities in the metropolitan region.

(3) To determine what patterns of residential population in the counties of the region will result from the probable future patterns of basic economic activities.

The findings will be of major significance for forecasting the size and distribution of future markets, population and land development as required in municipal and business planning, and for dispersal policy and administration.[10]

Fagin realized, as had Norton and Clark before, that more than narrowly physical considerations should receive attention, and he had perhaps a more sophisticated awareness than his predecessors of the technical problems and requirements of planning research. There was as yet no concrete hint of using the proposed study to refurbish RPA's languishing leadership role. This project was probably a precondition of a more active role.

ENTER THE FOUNDATIONS

It became obvious as these investigations progressed that foundation financing for this economic study would be required. The sums involved were too high for RPA's limited budget, and the special industry contributions that could be anticipated were not sufficient. Accordingly, proposals seeking foundation support were prepared.

Initial approaches to the Ford Foundation were not immediately successful. The Ford Foundation was at that time considering a large-scale program of grants for research on metropolitan affairs and could not act on RPA's request immediately. RPA then turned to the Rockefeller Brothers Fund. The Rockefeller Brothers Fund wished to see a study of this kind done but had doubts that RPA was the best group to do it. Norton sought to allay these doubts by citing the economic study that formed a part of the regional survey done in the 1920s. That study was not the regional plan but one of the prerequisites for such a plan.

This was the spirit of this current proposal; it would stand on its own feet and would be directly useful to many groups, both public and private. Also, Norton pointed out, RPA intended to retain a "top ranking industrial economist" to direct the technical aspects of the study. The study would be supervised by a committee of distinguished citizens, to be headed by Otto Nelson, vice-president of the New York Life Insurance Company and an RPA director. Norton tried to overcome fears that RPA's planning staff would be exercising control over a specifically economic study and that RPA was trying to produce another regional plan rather than an independently valuable economic study.

Although Norton expressed skepticism of subcontracting the study to another agency, Rockefeller Fund officials suggested that the Harvard Graduate School of Public Administration, headed by Dean Edward Mason, be brought into contact with RPA. About two weeks later, Henry Fagin met with representatives of the Rockefeller Brothers Fund and a group from the Harvard Graduate School of Public Administration.[11] Possibilities of cooperation and collaboration between RPA and the Harvard group were discussed. Fagin indicated RPA's desire to cooperate fully in whatever study the Fund might decide to finance. It was agreed that Mason would request a small grant to support two men in a three-month effort to analyze and re-define the project, reprice it, and recommend a form of project organization. On May 18, 1955, the directors of the Rockefeller Brothers Fund voted a $10,000 grant for this preliminary in-vestigation. Thus, the Fund brought the Harvard group into the project; the precise relationship of the Harvard group and RPA in the direction of the project was as yet not clear.

THE PROJECT MANAGEMENT COMMITTEE

The Rockefeller Fund had also suggested to Norton that RPA help organize a project management committee, which would be a broadly representative body of prominent citizens which could evaluate the proposal from the perspectives of several types of business and community involvement. The committee's job was to meet occasionally to review the work of the Harvard representatives doing the preliminary research design.[12] Members of this *ad hoc* group were to be chosen jointly by Mason, by the Rockefeller Brothers Fund, and by RPA. There was general agreement that this committee should be a broader-based and more prestigious group than could be drawn from the RPA board. Only four of the nineteen mem-bers of the committee were members of the RPA board—Otto Nelson, the committee chairman, Willard Hampton of the New York Telephone Company, Norton, and Osborne.

The committee was carefully chosen and well balanced. It included a newspaper executive, two bankers, two railroad presidents, a department store president, two economists, a real estate executive, a university chancellor, the city adminis-trator of New York City, the chairman of the Port of New York Authority, New Jersey's Commissioner of Conservation and Economic Development, the president of the Government Affairs Foundation, and a labor union official (RPA's first contact with organized labor) in addition to the four RPA board members.

The Harvard researchers completed their preliminary inquiry in the summer of 1955 and suggested a three-year study, estimated to cost about $500,000. The project management committee enthusiastically endorsed this recommendation but found the question of project organization to be more difficult.

The central issue was who, in the last analysis, would exercise direction and control of the project. The Rockefeller Brothers Fund, having brought the Harvard group into the study, was thought to favor an arrangement whereby a grant would be made to RPA, which would then engage the Harvard group to conduct the study, with Mason choosing the project director; the study would be directed by Harvard. This arrangement would produce a study made by Harvard for RPA.

There was substantial sentiment on the committee for local control and direction of the study. Some members urged an arrangement whereby control would be in the hands of a predominantly local group. This alternative envisioned a small top-level steering committee, which would include RPA representatives and a few other distinguished community figures.[13] In this arrangement, the grant would be made to RPA, which would then choose the project director, subject to steering committee approval. Thereafter the director would be directly responsible to the steering committee. This alternative would have given RPA a more substantial measure of control over the project.

After considerable discussion, the committee endorsed having the study made by Harvard for RPA. It was reported to the RPA board that "The Rockefeller Brothers Fund was interested in making a commitment to Harvard and . . . it seemed the part of wisdom to go along with the Fund's choice."[14]

Finally, in May, 1956, the Rockefeller Brothers Fund announced a grant of $240,000 to RPA for the economic study of the New York region. In the meantime, Fund officials had negotiated with the Ford Foundation to secure a matching grant of the same amount, so that $480,000 was made available for the study. A "memorandum of understanding" between RPA and the Harvard Graduate School of Public Administration formalized the arrangements recommended by the project management committee. A seven-member steering committee was created to review the study periodically, consisting of four representatives from Harvard and three from RPA. Economist Raymond Vernon was named by Harvard to direct the study.

Thus was the economic study of the region under way. The New York Metropolitan Region Study, as it came to be called, is probably the most significant research conducted on the New York region since the regional surveys of the 1920s. It was the beginning of a process of redefining RPA's program and role; consequently, the organizational arrangements are of more than casual interest. RPA leaders have often observed that this decision on organizational arrangements was one of most fateful decisions in the Association's recent history. They feared that a study directed by economists not responsible to RPA might well not follow through to the desired conclusion, that the economic projections would not be translated into physical projections useful for devising new regional development policies.

However, the project management committee and the Rockefeller Brothers Fund took the position they did because of doubts about what RPA would do with the venture. Also, with Fund officials and Harvard representatives participating in the selection, only four of RPA's board members were appointed to the nineteen-member project management committee. In effect, RPA's doctrines, competence, and status were being questioned at least by implication. Nevertheless, this study could provide the means for an organizational revival for RPA if RPA could take advantage of the opportunity, succeeding now where it had failed in the 1940s.

Development of New Programs

There were now important forces pushing RPA in the direction of a broader program and a revived leadership role. RPA's new leaders—Osborne, Fagin, and Norton—were eager for ambitious undertakings. The Ford Foundation, from the beginning of its involvement in the Harvard study, was keenly interested in the study being used for the mobilization of vigorous metropolitan community leadership that could provide an "action follow-up" to the project. The Ford Foundation was not interested merely in a new research program; it wanted to expend its funds in situations where effective civic leadership might be mobilized or encouraged. The organization of the Metropolitan Regional Council in 1956 testified to the growing awareness, at the official level of the interdependence of the region and suggested new and important roles for a metropolitan civic organization. Toward the end of the Harvard study, the advisory committee to that study, a top-level group of regional leaders (Table 4), manifested great interest in a follow-up of the Harvard study but had nagging doubts whether RPA as then constituted was suited for the necessary leadership job. Thus, there were stronger incentives than ever before for RPA to revise its program and assert a more vigorous leadership role.

In discussing possible follow-up programs after completion of the economic study, Ford Foundation officials urged RPA to apply for a small grant to engage in self-study and reassessment of its organizational role. The Foundation suggested that the staff visit several other metropolitan areas, observe the public and private agencies concerned with regional development policies, and use the insights gained from this observation in

TABLE 4

MEMBERSHIP OF ADVISORY COMMITTEE TO
NEW YORK METROPOLITAN REGION STUDY

Amory H. Bradford	Vice-president and business manager, N.Y. *Times*
W. Nelson Bump	Regional vice-president, American Airlines
William A. M. Burden	William A. M. Burden & Co.
S. Sloan Colt	Director, Bankers Trust Co.
Robert G. Cowan	President, National Newark & Essex Banking Co.
Cleo Craig	Chairman of the board, American Telephone & Telegraph Co.
Thomas C. Desmond	State Senator, Newburgh, N.Y.
James Felt	Chairman, N.Y. City Planning Commission
Luther Gulick	President, Institute of Public Administration
Willard G. Hampton	Executive vice-president, N.Y. Telephone Co.
Paul M. Herzog	Executive vice-president, American Arbitration Association
L. Clinton Hoch	Partner, Fantus Factory Location Service
Donald V. Lowe	Commissioner, Port of N.Y. Authority
Isador Lubin	Franklin D. Roosevelt Foundation
Lawrence C. Marshall	Executive vice-president, Chase Manhattan Bank
Edward S. Mason	Dean, Graduate School of Public Administration, Harvard University
Stacy May	Economist, International Basic Economy Corp.
Frank C. Moore	President, Government Affairs Foundation
Thomas A. Morgan	Director, U.S. Industries
Otto L. Nelson	Vice-president, N.Y. Life Insurance Co.
A. L. Nickerson	President, Socony Mobil Oil Co.
C. McKim Norton	Executive vice-president, Regional Plan Association
Harold S. Osborne	Consulting engineer, Upper Montclair, N.J.
William S. Paley	Chairman of the board, Columbia Broadcasting System
H. Bruce Palmer	President, Mutual Benefit Life Insurance Co.
William S. Renchard	Executive vice-president, Chemical Bank N.Y. Trust Co.
David Rockefeller	Vice-chairman of the board, Chase Manhattan Bank
Earl B. Schwulst	President, Bowery Savings Bank
Jack I. Straus	Chairman of the board, R. H. Macy & Co.
Harry Van Arsdale, Jr.	President, N.Y. City Central Labor Council
Ralph Walker	Partner, Voorhees, Walker, Smith, Smith, & Haines (architects)
Ralph J. Watkins	Director of Economic Studies, Brookings Institution
Walter H. Wheeler, Jr.	President, Pitney-Bowes (postage meters)

a reappraisal of RPA's program. A grant of $25,000 was made to RPA for this purpose early in 1957.

The Ford Foundation was therefore inviting RPA to evaluate itself critically and to revise its commitments to the extent necessary for the assumption of a larger role. Realizing that innovation is more likely when key members of the organization are freed from concern with day-to-day operations, the Foundation made it possible for Fagin and Norton to devote the bulk of their time to this study. This grant, plus the prospect of eventual large-scale Foundation support for a future program, was thus a very attractive stimulus to innovation.

The ultimate result of this study [15] was a program for constructing several alternative physical models of the region as it might appear some years hence, all of them feasible, with analysis of the costs and decisions necessary to bring each model into being. One such model would be provided by the Harvard study, which would depict the shape the region would take if present development trends were not altered. It was hoped that large-scale participation of civic, business, and governmental leaders could be secured in studying the models and deciding which was preferable. It was assumed that participation in the choice of the model to be achieved would lead to promotion of the policies needed to bring that alternative into being. In this way, a new regional plan was to be developed and executed. This proposal was priced at about $2 million beyond RPA's anticipated income, and it was estimated that it would require about $3⅓ million to complete.[16]

No particular qualitative shift of emphasis in RPA's program was contemplated at that time. The proposed new program called more for expansion than revision of RPA's priorities and operations. In addition to designing alternative models of regional development and generating a broad consensus on desirable growth patterns, the staff recommended strengthening RPA's role in planning education by assistance to colleges and universities and by establishing a bureau of regional statistics.[17] Both of these latter recommendations keenly interested Fagin, who was much concerned about the adequacy of planning research and the competencies of professional planners. In general, then, the new program proposals did not involve the explicit modification of any of RPA's commitments.

AMBIGUITIES OF THE PROPOSAL

Certain features of the proposal drafted early in 1958 are significant as evidence of a gradual change in RPA's conceptions of planning. The first major phase of the project was the delineation of a small number of alternative models of regional development. RPA's staff, far more than the planners of the 1920s, realized that any model or plan of regional development would embody certain goals and preferences and deny others. Attuned to positivist criticism of planning, the staff did not advocate a duplication of the experience of the 1920s, where a plan based on the implicit value judgments of the planners was presented without an adequate analysis of those value choices underlying the physical conclusions. It was proposed instead that the study give systematic consideration to criteria for evaluating the alternative models. This involved not only economic criteria, which might be suggested by the Harvard study, but social and political criteria as well. This was admittedly a complex problem; the staff saw the problem in three stages:

The problem of evaluation is inherently difficult. In respect to regional patterns it involves: first, identification of the classes of issues that warrant weighing; second, means for measurement within a given classification or criterion; and third, means for weighing advantages and disadvantages with regard to one criterion against considerations related to different criteria. To some extent, the dollar may be employed as a common denominator. It may be possible to place approximate dollar values on such matters as the quality of living quarters or the time-saving accruing from a toll bridge or suburban railroad where alternative and cheaper routes are available. There are other values, however, which are not reflected in the price mechanism, yet are given serious weight by people in the making of their decisions. Some means, moreover, must be developed to enable one combination of values to be considered against another combination of values.[18]

There seems to be ambiguity here as to whether some planners' version of a "hedonistic calculus" could be designed which would "objectively" measure and compare these considerations, yielding one optimum alternative, or whether the study would simply identify and underscore the nature of the choices involved so that the groups participating in the study would have a clearer conception of just what the underlying issues were.

If it was believed that a scheme of measurement could be worked out and a "one best way" identified accordingly, the proposal represents a more sophisticated version of planning doctrine, though not necessarily a fundamental revision of it. This would involve essentially a repetition of a 1929-type plan with a volume on a calculus of value choices added. The major change would be making the underlying choices explicit but not necessarily questioning the inherent objectivity of the choices.

On the other hand, if it were thought that this section of the study would simply identify and clarify what the basic choices among various goals were, a different kind of plan and organizational role would be involved. It would then become necessary to put the findings of the study before a wide variety of relevant groups and interests so that they might become sensitized to the issues involved and begin to analyze their own preferences. The proposal called for the creation of a broadly representative "committee on the region" and for the periodic participation of the Metropolitan Regional Council, relevant state and local agencies, and various civic, business, and labor groups. The study hoped to

encourage a high degree of consensus among the public and private agencies whose combined efforts shape the region as to regional policies to be followed to meet the problems arising from the region's growth.[19]

The mobilization of these groups and their deliberation becomes a crucial matter, the crux of the entire effort, by this interpretation. If, however, the planners produce a latter-day Benthamite calculus, this mobilization of interests becomes an ancillary activity of "selling" relevant groups on the merits of the planner-preferred alternative. Put perhaps oversimply, the question was whether the basic choices would be made at the drawing board or at the conference table. That the staff leaned in the direction of the conference table is suggested by their understanding that "in the last analysis the choice among alternatives must be based on scales of values and expressed through appropriate political processes," a statement which suggests a recognition of the complexity of the political process and the subjectivity of the value choices involved.

The proposal adds that "It is anticipated, however, that the research done would greatly assist these political processes to take place." [20] This was the first suggestion that an essential part of RPA's mission was to stimulate the development of regional political processes. Depending on how this aspect of the proposal was interpreted in practice, RPA might continue on more or less traditional paths, or it might assume a stronger leadership role and put the organization of regional leadership on a par with its commitment to research.

FOUNDATION REACTION

The Ford Foundation's interest in metropolitan affairs had been an important stimulus to RPA's search for a new program. Foundation officials consistently stressed the importance of a strong local financial base and the creation of more substantial resources of civic leadership in metropolitan areas. The Foundation's viewpoint has been summarized by one of its spokesmen:

As the Ford Foundation has sharpened its focus in the field of public affairs, its program has tended to become increasingly action —rather than research—oriented. And where research projects have received support, they have been intimately related to action programs.[21]

In informal conversations between Ford Foundation officials and RPA leaders, RPA was encouraged to revise its proposal by giving more systematic attention to the organization of a broader leadership and financial base. Foundation officials apparently thought that in practice RPA's proposal might amount to making a new regional plan first, then "selling it" to the committee on the region. RPA now faced the same choice that had confronted the planners of the 1920s. Should the organization of regional leadership be made an equally important task alongside making "the largest and finest plans"? Or should the organization of leadership come later, and be given a subordinate, secondary status? The Ford Foundation seemed unwilling to commit a large sum to an organization that had not clearly developed a strong leadership commitment.

After these conversations with Ford Foundation representatives, one of the RPA participants reported to the RPA board, noting

a change of emphasis of interest of the Foundation staff away from the more technical elements of the proposed regional policy development program and greater emphasis on its educational aspects. The Foundation also expects civic leadership to be highly organized in the regions in which it makes grants. Finally, the Foundation always wished to make sure that the organization which it supports has the financial strength to carry on after the termination of the period of the grants.[22]

This was a potent stimulus for organizational change, since it was clear that RPA could not get enough additional nonfoundation support to finance the kind of program it contemplated.

RPA RESPONDS

The immediate task now facing RPA's leadership was to develop another proposal. In a subsequent meeting of the RPA executive committee, the question of how far RPA should go in the restoration of a leadership role was the primary subject of discussion.[23] Although some expressed interest in a vigorous role, most did not wish RPA to become overly aggressive. The majority sentiment seemed to be that RPA should not become a "political pressure group" but should "produce factual data on which public discussion can then be based."

On the basis of this agreement, the staff and key board members went to work on a revised proposal. This advocated discussion of the findings of the Harvard economic study among a variety of leaders drawn from government, business, and civic organizations.[24] The object of these deliberations was described in a memorandum to the board:

It is expected through this program that we would achieve an appreciation on the part of the leaders of the region of the need of most or all of the program of analysis of alternative development patterns which has been prepared by our staff.[25]

The ultimate result, hopefully, would be a new, informed policy consensus among important public and private agencies capable of affecting regional development. The specific end in view for this particular project, however, was not that policy consensus but convincing these groups of the need for RPA's previously proposed planning project. At this stage, RPA was trying to respond to the Foundation's standards with a minimal reconsideration of its traditional balance between research and leadership.

Although RPA viewed this new proposal as only a first step in a revitalized RPA, it was unable to attract foundation support. It would have to move farther in the direction of a broad leadership role to get the desired support. A serious and possibly far-reaching reconsideration of organizational commitments and priorities seemed in order.

RPA's leaders understood their situation. Osborne was eager to get the Association officially committed to a broader role. He was enthusiastically supported by Fagin, who had just returned from a six-month leave of absence, during which he had served as Ford Foundation Research Professor in the Department of Political Science at the University of California at Berkeley. Fagin had returned to RPA with more specific notions of what directions the broadening of RPA might take. Norton, of course, had tried since 1940 to restore to RPA the breadth and vision of its founders. Osborne, with the help of Fagin and Norton, drafted an eight-point statement which summarized some of the trends implicit in RPA's recent thinking. These were not completely new directions but tendencies already present which would now be made explicit, be officially recognized, and be formally adopted as part of RPA's basic program commitments:

1. The scope of the work is broadening. The Association is concerned now not merely with physical plans but broadly with plans necessary to provide for the proper handling of matters of a regional nature. This includes organizational as well as physical aspects.

2. In recent years research has been a large part of the program of the Association and probably always will form a part of it. It is proposed, however, that for the years ahead major emphasis be placed on the application of the information provided by recent analysis.

3. In studying applications the Association will work primarily with other groups, particularly "action agencies," stimulating in them an appreciation of the regional nature of many problems and the importance of coordinating their activities. The emphasis in the work of the Association has shifted from the drawing board to the conference table.

4. The Association will work in closer cooperation than heretofore with government, particularly with the Metropolitan Regional Council and with the respective administrations of the three states.

5. The Association has a continuing interest in expressing its opinions on specific projects when these are of regional importance. The Association should continue to do this. However, in view of the magnitude of the general program outlined, it will for the present have to be very selective in the choice of specific projects to be studied in order not to interfere unduly with the general program.

6. The Association must develop a broader support from the

community. The research phases of the work here have largely been supported by foundations. It is appropriate that the Association be more largely supported by the community itself.

7. All of this points up the need which we have already recognized for getting as soon as possible at the head of the Association someone who is currently well known, active, and influential in the business community.

8. The program calls for increased participation of the members of the Board of Directors in various ways.[26]

This was possibly the most significant policy statement in RPA's history. It reemphasized the inadequacy of physical planning alone, a point which Norton had been making since 1940. Its focus on application of research results rather than research per se and the expressed need to relate RPA more closely to government agencies represented a renewed interest in policy development. The "scattered shot" nature of the Association's program since the decline of the 1929 Plan as a focus was rejected, and a new general program was envisioned. The need for increased status and support was reiterated. This was a statement in the spirit of the Association's early leaders.

The board adopted Osborne's policy statement with some enthusiasm. Although a few argued that the statement was too unspecific and represented too much of an "ivory tower" approach, most were highly favorable to a more active policy and leadership role. Adoption of this statement by the board did not by itself constitute a revision of organizational commitments. If this action was not followed through in terms of RPA's organization and working program, it would ultimately come to naught, as had some earlier declarations purporting to chart new courses.

The Metropolitan Regional Council

RPA was no longer standing alone as a regional institution. In 1956, Mayor Wagner had called a conference of the elected chief executives of the counties and municipalities in the region. The origins of this step are not entirely clear. Some have suggested that RPA had some role in this; RPA leaders, however, state that RPA probably had little to do with that decision and that, in any event, credit belongs primarily to Wagner. Whatever the origins of the idea, it was more successful than anyone had probably imagined. Officials from twenty-one of the twenty-two counties [27] in the region responded, and in 1957 the members put the group on a permanent organizational basis and began to take official positions on pending legislation in Congress. The unity of the region was becoming less a planners' abstraction and more a tangible reality.

The new group was warmly received by RPA. In 1958 RPA and the Metropolitan Regional Council (MRC) engaged in joint sponsorship of a study, financed by the Old Dominion, Taconic, and Victoria Foundations, of park, recreation, and open-space needs in the region. It was conducted by the RPA staff under the general direction of a carefully chosen steering committee. Its co-chairmen were Griffith E. Harris, First Selectman of Greenwich, Connecticut, and chairman of the Council's Recreation Committee, and Otto Nelson of RPA. Other members were John G. Baker, President Emeritus of the National Audubon Society; H. P. Davidson, board member of the National Recreation Association; William E. Roach, Jr., Planning Director for Somerset County, New Jersey, and chairman of the Metropolitan Council of Planning Agencies; and C. Mc-Kim Norton of RPA.

RPA was highly pleased with the organizational formula used here—joint RPA-MRC sponsorship plus a few prominent citizens active in the field concerned. The results reinforced RPA's confidence. The report is said to have influenced the drafting of federal open-space legislation, and several of its specific recommendations were soon carried out. RPA leaders frequently point to this open-space study as a leading example of the results that can be achieved through carefully designed cooperative ventures. At the same time the study helped establish amicable relationships between the two regional organizations and encouraged RPA's acceptance of the policy statement it had just adopted.

None the less, RPA had traditionally shied away from "metropolitan supergovernment." In view of its general disinclination to tamper with governmental structure, its relation to the MRC posed a problem. At the same time, to encourage the evolution of the Council to a position of stability and permanence and to strengthen RPA's position as an element of the Council's constituency, it seemed desirable that RPA go further than collaboration on studies with the Council.

There were, then, several reasons why RPA needed to clarify the role of the MRC and RPA's relation to it. Meanwhile, the Council had created a committee on the future of the Council to explore possible avenues of institutional development. Proposals of possible official status and even minor taxing powers were being bruited about. In the context of these conditions, then, RPA's executive committee in the fall of 1958 authorized the president to appoint a committee on metropolitan governmental matters with this assignment:

To prepare a report which would be made available to the Regional Plan Association, to the Metropolitan Regional Council, and to the public on governmental organizations for administering the affairs of the Tri-State Metropolitan Region, with special reference to the Future of the Metropolitan Regional Council.[28]

Such a committee was appointed under the chairmanship of Wallace S. Sayre, Eaton Professor of Public Administration at Columbia University.[29]

The Sayre committee's report was submitted in January, 1959. The report incisively and emphatically stressed the absolute necessity for a "central general-purpose official leadership institution" [30] in the region. However, the committee did not propose to convert the MRC into a kind of general regional government. Its proposals were modest but highly significant:

The Committee, therefore recommends:

First: that the Metropolitan Regional Council acquire full legal status as a regional agency. Such status would be conferred by (1) the enactment of identical statutes in Connecticut, New Jersey, and New York establishing the Council as a tri-state agency, and (2) the approval in the United States Congress of an interstate compact recognizing the Council as a regional agency.

Second: that the Council improve its organization to carry out these new leadership responsibilities, especially by adding to its present resources a small full-time, talented and experienced secretariat.

Third: that the Council, when thus possessed of full legal status and a capable staff, focus its attention and its energies increasing (1) upon the discovery and identification of the Region's potential for growth, (2) upon the precise formulation of regional goals which will maximize the usefulness of the Region's human and material resources, (3) upon the careful analysis of the region's problems, and (4) upon the development of specific recommendations for solutions to the Region's difficulties.[31]

The general theme of the report was that the development of an official leadership institution was the region's greatest single need:

It needs to be emphasized and reemphasized that solutions to these specific problems of the Region, urgent as they now are or may become, are less crucial to the long-range future of the Region than is the careful shaping and development of the Metropolitan Regional Council as the central general-purpose official leadership institution of the Tri-State Metropolitan Region.[32]

The concerns of the Council were regarded broadly:

The Council has defined its assignment as one of broad regional leadership, concerned with the analysis and solution of any problem recognized as regional in its character by members of the Council.[33]

RPA's role was noted:

The Region also has several regional citizen and professional associations of great usefulness. Among these, The Regional Plan Association is the oldest, the most consistently active, and has the widest range of interests. These non-governmental associations have a highly important function to perform in the future growth of the Region. But they cannot realize their full potential of usefulness unless there also exists an official regional agency, composed of elected public officials, to which the citizen associations may present their proposals.[34]

The MRC could thus serve as an audience for RPA. If RPA was to serve as a civic counterpart to the Council, actively co-operating with it and stimulating it, RPA's interests would presumably have to be as broad as those of the Council.

The Metropolitan Press

Another indication of increasing general concern with regional problems was the heightened interest of the metropolitan press, particularly the New York *Times.* From the early 1950s, the *Times* was increasingly aware of its own inevitable involvement with regional problems. Like utilities and some other businesses, the *Times* was a regional institution and could not escape direct concern with regional problems. Metropolitan problems became a major area of concern for the *Times,* a concern reflected not only on the editorial pages but in the news space and coverage given to regional problems as well. The RPA was given probably the best press coverage it had ever enjoyed since the initial reporting of the Regional Plan of 1929.

This concern has spilled over into the other major New York daily newspapers and has also been quite pronounced in many suburban papers. This increased concern of the press was not a pressure of a direct sort on RPA, but it made acceptance of a passive research role a much less attractive choice. Much of the metropolitan press was making itself available as a major resource of regional leadership, inviting vigorous initiatives by civic groups like RPA.

In 1959 RPA invited Amory Bradford, then vice-president

and business manager of the *Times,* to become president of RPA. Bradford, a longtime friend of Norton and a member of the project management committee and the advisory committee to the Harvard study, was approached by several RPA directors but hesitated initially because of the time the RPA post would require. The officers of the *Times* indicated that they considered the RPA post important and deserving of the time that would be involved, so Bradford accepted, spending considerable time with RPA over the next three years. RPA thus secured another highly effective president, who presided over major organizational innovations.

Thus, the environment was changing. Broad public concern with metropolitan problems was increasing. The Ford Foundation and other major foundations were committed to the study of urban and regional problems, stimulating RPA to develop new policies and revive its leadership role. The rise of the MRC and the keen interest of much of the metropolitan press assured RPA of a growing audience. All these factors combined to provide RPA with its greatest opportunity to develop new policies since the days of the Regional Plan. Still other external stimuli were soon to arise which would make the rehabilitation of an RPA leadership role even more urgent. These forces, and RPA's responses, are the subject of the following chapter.

CHAPTER VI

The Rehabilitation
of Purpose: II

The forces and events described in the preceding chapter provided new incentives and opportunities for RPA to develop new goals and to assume a more vigorous leadership role. These environmental changes and internal pressures were more nearly inducements which promised rewards for successful innovation than they were imperatives which threatened RPA's organizational status if RPA did not alter its commitments. RPA could, if it wished, decline to meet the requirements of the Ford Foundation. It might thereby miss a unique opportunity for organizational development, but its very survival would not be jeopardized. There were, however, other forces that were more imperative. As a result, innovation became less a possible alternative that might or might not be deliberately chosen and more a necessity for the maintenance of RPA's institutional position.

The Advisory Committee

Before the New York Metropolitan Region Study was underway, Harvard University's Graduate School of Public Administration and RPA recruited an advisory committee to oversee the study. The project management committee that reported to the Rockefeller Brothers Fund late in 1955 had recommended a committee "representing the groups within the metropolitan area that are most likely to be the users of the final product and others most competent to advise on various aspects of the project." [1]

A 33-man committee (Table 4 in the last chapter) was then set up. Several RPA directors, especially Otto Nelson, RPA vice-president and chairman of the Project Management Committee, and Luther Gulick, president of the Institute of Public Administration and recently elected to RPA's board, were active in recruiting members. Raymond Vernon, director of the study, and others of the Harvard group also had a hand in some of the selections, perhaps to open up important data sources. Thirteen members had served on the project management committee, and nine were members of the RPA board. Of these nine RPA directors, four were RPA officers—Harold Osborne, McKim Norton, Otto Nelson, and Willard Hampton; four others were very recent additions to the board—H. Bruce Palmer, who came on the board in 1954, and Luther Gulick, Frank Moore, and Ralph Walker, who came on in 1956; the other was Earl Schwulst, president of the Bowery Savings Bank, who had been a Board member since 1941. (Three more members of the committee—Amory Bradford, William Renchard, and Harry Van Arsdale—joined the RPA board after the work of the Committee was well under way.)

This highly prestigious committee met ten times during the course of the study and in 1959, shortly before publication of the first of the Harvard study's nine volumes, began to consider what report it would make to the RPA board. The committee had heard periodic reports by the study's staff and was aware of the general conclusions that the published volumes would reveal. At what was to have been its final meeting in April, 1959,

Several members of the Advisory Committee expressed the view that steps should be taken promptly to create an organization which would carry forward the next stages of the work for which the Metropolitan Region Study should provide the foundation. It was felt that the first major task would be the dissemination of the findings of the study to interested agencies and individuals through-out the metropolitan region. While this was being accomplished, and as an awareness of the problems was created, it would be neces-sary to provide a form of organization which could pull together interest groups throughout the Region in formulating plans and carrying them out. . . . It was agreed that the Advisory Committee should not complete its work until it had done its best to block out a program along these lines.[2]

Consequently, two further meetings were held where these mat-ters were considered.

The concern to see the Harvard study followed by an effec-tive program producing and promoting new guidelines for re-gional development was self-generated by the committee; this had not been part of its original assignment. The members had been strikingly impressed by the trends the Harvard study re-vealed and were convinced of the need for strong leadership on a continuing basis to produce a better region than the one en-visioned by these trends.

The advisory committee examined the organization of com-munity leadership in other regions, including Pittsburgh, Phil-adelphia, Cleveland, and New Haven. The differences in the size and complexity of these regions and the New York region were apparent. There was general recognition that "the" mon-olithic decision-making elite could not be assembled, because it probably did not exist. There was a need, however, to bring together a small number of leading figures from business, labor, education, and civic affairs to lead in the choice of policies to shape regional growth in desirable patterns. There was general agreement that a "widely representative" group of the re-gion's "top leadership" be established as a committee on the development of the region. The committee apparently felt that RPA as constituted at that time did not have the status in the community or the commitment to leadership to do the job en-visioned by the committee. It may also be possible that some members of the committee viewed the proposal for a new regional leadership institution as a spur to RPA to move decisively in this direction.

There was a difference of opinion on the timing of the establishment of this new group. Some felt the task was so urgent that the committee should be launched immediately. Others, including some RPA board members, were more cautious. There was some concern about appearing to act preemptively, before the region was generally aware of the need for new policy choices in these areas: hasty action might damage the new committee's image.

RPA's leaders were also less confident than the advisory committee that the Harvard study was a sufficient basis for developing a program. The study did not follow through to an analysis of land uses, which RPA regarded as fundamental for devising intelligent development policies. Furthermore, since RPA had been largely separated from the Harvard study, the RPA staff at that time was largely unfamiliar with the details of the study. It was believed that without a sounder research basis for policy development than the Harvard study by itself provided, the committee on the development of the region would soon founder. From their background of experience in this area, the RPA leaders had a greater awareness of the great complexity of the region's problems and a more sophisticated awareness of what had to be known in order to plan wisely.

A memorandum from RPA's new president and executive director, Amory Bradford and John Keith, urged that creation of the committee on the development of the region be deferred for one year. In the meantime, a temporary committee should be set up to identify and conduct further needed research and plan the organization of the more permanent action-oriented committee on the development of the region.[3] In another memorandum to the advisory committee two weeks later, the RPA leaders urged that "The real need would appear to be to develop a continuing, close relationship between the Regional Plan Association and the proposed Temporary Committee on the Region." [4]

The final report of the advisory committee, presented to the RPA board on October 5, 1959, made two recommendations:

1. Dissemination of the material in the Metropolitan Region Study, in a manner which will lead to intensive discussion throughout the Region and an evaluation of the findings as they affect different areas and institutions.
2. Establishment of a Steering Committee charged with the responsibility within one year of recommending the detailed organization of a widely representative Committee on the Development of the Region. This Steering Committee should also play a major role in the dissemination of the studies, so that it will keep in close touch with community reaction as it develops. [5]

Although the advisory group had accepted the proposed delay in creating the top-level regional committee, it expressed some reservations about this:

There is added strength in the recommended, two-stage approach; there also is inherent danger. The proposed gradual build-up will mean that the timing of the changeover from provisional to full-fledged Committee effort is crucial. There will be a moment when the initiative must be firmly seized before the Region, without leadership, fractionalizes itself in its thinking concerning the Study. [6]

The report concludes with some general comments about the kind of planning program the Committee envisioned:

Planning and development can be thought of as a four-stage process: (1) defining goals, (2) surveying past, present, and future development, (3) making plans, and (4) implementing plans. Generally, city planning has concentrated on stages two and three. Perhaps the most ambitious effort to date encompassing stages one and two was that made in advance of formalizing the "Regional Plan of New York and Its Environs." The Harvard Study represents an important extension of that process concentrating on stage two.

The next major assignment for the RPA, as we see it, is that of developing public awareness and understanding of regional goals— in other words, acting in the almost uncharted area of stage one. Certainly the program of the Steering Committee, and subsequently of the Committee on the Development of the Region, is of a different scope, if not a different order, than that undertaken thirty years ago. Of necessity, the community must participate in the development of its own goals so that they are, in fact, goals upon which all the community can unite. The job of creating the goals cannot be done by a small, pilot body, by law, or other fiat. The community must be led by voluntary civic leadership to coalesce around common objectives.[7]

A new set of policy guidelines based on a newly generated consensus on regional goals was to be brought about, but a replication of the 1929 Plan was not in order. There is perhaps a suggestion here that the new machinery of a steering committee and a committee on the development of the region is necessary because RPA was perhaps too closely wedded to its past commitments and experience to handle the broader tasks that the advisory committee perceived. This was not a surprising position. The study to which this committee was advisory was deliberately set up independently of RPA. The Ford Foundation had tried to push RPA toward new directions but had not been satisfied with the proposals put forward to follow the Harvard study, and the RPA board did not possess the stature of the projected committee. In short, a new task, beyond RPA's traditional role, was envisioned. Consequently, new organizational machinery was required.

What would RPA's role be in this projected state of affairs? RPA leaders saw several alternatives at this juncture. RPA might become a publicity bureau for the dissemination of the findings of the Harvard study. This would undermine its planning and research functions and distort the conception it had developed which viewed the Harvard study as a basis for a new program rather than as an end in itself. If this occurred, initiative with respect to policies and actions to be proposed would pass to the new committee.

A second alternative, one which seemed implicit in some of the advisory committee's deliberations, was for RPA to become the research arm, or staff secretariat, to the new group. Should this happen, RPA might lose its identity in a subordinate role and forfeit whatever reputation it had won as a leadership institution. Both of these alternatives would clearly subordinate RPA to the committee on the development of the region, and the survival of a thirty-year old institution might be placed in jeopardy.

The leaders of RPA's staff, with knowledge gained from both observation and long experience, realized the difficulty of maintaining sustained active participation in any civic enterprise by top-level leaders in any institutional complex, whether business, labor, or whatever. It was possible that such a committee might come into being in the advisory committee's initial burst of enthusiasm, compete with RPA for funds and dry up its financial base, and lose interest after two or three years, leaving a weakened and impoverished RPA. To subordinate RPA to a probably temporary group that might not think in terms of RPA's long-term interests seemed to jeopardize the resources of permanence and continuity that RPA had maintained through years of some tribulation. RPA had never been happy with the organizational arrangements of the Harvard study and would not wish to repeat this now on a larger scale.

On the other hand, RPA was not necessarily opposed to the creation of an elite committee if the committee existed for the sake of RPA rather than vice versa. It could be a valuable adjunct to a broadened and expanded RPA. In any event, the most pressing need at that moment was for substantial organizational development of RPA. The optimum alternative would be for RPA to rise to the leadership role envisioned by the advisory committee.

RPA Reacts

After the appearance of the advisory committee report, the RPA board had an extended discussion of RPA's future role.[8] One director argued, "Why organize a Committee on the Development of the Region? Why shouldn't a strengthened RPA do the job?" Another noted that it was "imperative that the steering committee be tied tightly to RPA so that there could exist no possibility of developing two staffs and, as a consequence, a fund-raising conflict arising detrimental to RPA." It was suggested that the steering committee make its report to the RPA board, rather than to some third party. RPA, another noted, was inviting serious trouble if it did not control the steering committee and its recommendations. According to the minutes, "there was unanimous agreement . . . that RPA must retain its leadership."

The board adopted the advisory committee report "in principle." It did so with misgivings about the specific recommendations in the report. If RPA wished to avert this impending threat to its organizational status, it would have to produce an alternative program for strengthening RPA.

THE COATES REPORT

This alternative response was not long in coming. Shortly after the board had considered the advisory committee report, the Association, at the instigation of John Keith, engaged the services of a consulting firm, Charles B. Coates and Company, to analyze RPA and help draft a working plan of operation for it. It was necessary to block out some new goals and procedures for RPA, but none of the earlier efforts to turn the organization to new directions had been completely successful. More was needed now than a general policy statement; a specific program of operation was required. Keith therefore introduced a new wrinkle in RPA's efforts for innovation by bringing in an outside consultant to assist in this task.

The use of a management and public relations consultant was a technique thoroughly familiar to the business executives on the board, and bringing in a consultant was calculated to make the resulting recommendations more acceptable to the board. Coates worked closely with Keith and Norton, and they jointly participated in the drafting of the report to the board. Their report is unambiguously addressed to the organizational problems posed by the advisory committee report and to the preservation of RPA's institutional position.

According to the report, the key element in the situation is the lack of a new Regional Plan. Getting such a plan is the top priority, and action-oriented activities at that time would be premature. This represents an emphasis and a scale of priorities different from the advisory committee's report, which had envisioned the organization of regional leadership as the top-priority task. To the advisory committee the central problem was to develop a leadership institution that could successfully support a new set of regional policies. RPA's approach was more traditional and more cautious.

Because of the priority of new plans, RPA's first task was to undertake research to translate the findings of the Harvard study into a physical projection of what the region would be like in 1985 unless appropriate action were taken to offset existing trends. The immediate task was what came to be called a "projections project."

The priority given to this project was also a reflection of the RPA staff's dissatisfaction with the Harvard study as a platform for RPA. The staff had originally wanted an economic study for the sake of such a projection; the foundations involved and the Harvard group were more interested in an economic study for its own sake. As a result, RPA did not get the end product it wanted, and much of the research done was of little direct benefit to RPA. RPA thus explicitly took issue with the implied position of the advisory committee that the study was a sufficient basis for a new program.

The second recommendation of the consultant's report likewise was a response to the view that the Harvard study, as it stood, was not the end product RPA needed. The advisory committee had recommended that the proposed steering committee disseminate the findings of the study. In RPA's view, those findings were not ready-made for widespread dissemination. The staff recognized that extensive press coverage had been given to the appearance of each of the study volumes, but RPA had not been able to control the timing of these releases and thus had not been able to use them to maximum advantage. Further, a single exposure of the public to each of these volumes was not presumed to have made a great impact. Therefore, the report recommended that "The factual findings of the Harvard Study must be 'boiled down' and placed within the reach of many readers in handy form." [9]

This digest and explanation of the Harvard study was the first requirement of the projected information program. There was a further need to decide "How many of what sort of people is it important to reach with the digested facts of the Harvard Study—and when?" [10] From the outset, RPA had recognized the need to influence various community elites; it had not tried to be a mass organization. The consultant's report continued this emphasis.[11] It suggested that the information program be directed at "primary decision-makers." These included public officials, major business executives, civic, labor, and educational leaders, and others. Just as Frederic Delano has eschewed primary reliance on the mass media in the 1920s, the report placed priorities on meetings, seminars, speeches, and personal contact. The mass media were not to be left out, but they were not the prime focus of the program. The report thus reaffirmed the early conception of leadership through influencing a relatively small group of leaders of key elites.

This mobilization of leaders was to proceed cautiously. The report reminded the directors that the information effort could only be directed at "creation of awareness" of regional development problems, since RPA lacked a concrete program. Lacking at this stage both a general awareness of regional problems and a set of specific action proposals, the advisory committee's recommendation that an elite committee be set up in one year seemed premature. The RPA staff was convinced that an ade-

quate research and information basis for a strong leadership
role would take longer to establish.

The report's third general recommendation was the creation,
as a part of RPA, of a series of specialized developmental committees, drawn primarily from the RPA board and the advisory
committee. These committees would assist in carrying out the
information program and in recruiting broader support for
RPA. Finally, armed with new projections and plans and supported by a carefully designed expanded information program,
RPA could begin to think about implementation of its new
program. The report concluded: "It is quite conceivable that
an expanded RPA, working from a concrete conception of coordinated regional development, can itself take on the implementation job." [12] Consequently, the committee on the development of the region might be wholly unnecessary.

The report also urged RPA to move toward an expansion of
its services to business and promotion of the economic competitiveness of the region. RPA, the report noted, "is not well
known to the business community generally and it may take
some time to correct this." [13] To overcome this, it was important for RPA to sell itself to potential supporters by demon-
strating its relevance to the contributor's own interests. This
was not a new theme; Charles Norton used arguments based on
long-term economies to justify the Regional Plan, and RPA
had always provided some data and information to some of its
members. It was now suggested that these functions should receive a higher priority of attention and emphasis.

Another portent of changing emphasis was spelled out in a
memorandum by McKim Norton concerning the proposed projections project. This memorandum was prepared while the
consultant's report was being drafted. Norton explicitly differentiates RPA's proposed program from the kind of effort represented in the 1929 Regional Plan:

It should be pointed out, however, that the formation of comprehensive, long-range regional development policies comparable

in scope to the original "Regional Plan of New York and Its Environs" is another and much bigger undertaking to which the projections are simply a preface.

It is clear to us that the long-range work must be done largely with public financing and under public auspices. It is equally clear that, without stimulation and direction from a citizens regional organization, it will not be done on a regional basis at all. . . . Large-scale federal (and some state and city) funds are available today to meet many of the needs of the regional research and planning—provided they are directed to properly organized studies.[14]

RPA was no less insistent than ever that comprehensive planning be done, but the major tasks were now conceded to government. RPA would serve as part of the constituency of the governmental agencies concerned with these planning efforts. RPA need not attempt the entire research and planning job itself, as the Committee on the Regional Plan had done in the 1920s.

This narrowing of RPA's commitment to undertake comprehensive planning was consistent with the expansion of service functions and increasing economic emphasis. The less global research commitment implied here was accompanied by Norton's declaration that the assertion of regional leadership was now "a primary goal." [15] Although the temporal priority of research was reiterated, consideration of the information and leadership tasks was not postponed pending completion of further studies. Thus, RPA's leaders contemplated increased emphasis on leadership, the region's economy, information services, and a narrower role for RPA in comprehensive planning.

The consultant's report was adopted with enthusiasm by the RPA board early in 1960. Many expressed great satisfaction that RPA was making an effective positive response to the challenges before it. An even more concrete response was soon to be generated.

A Program Is Drafted

While the consultant's report was in preparation, RPA once again approached the Ford Foundation, this time seeking funds to carry out the proposed projections project. Several other foundations were also approached in this connection. When RPA's president met with Ford Foundation officials early in April, 1960, he was advised that the Foundation had strong interests beyond the projections proposal and the planned information program sketched in the consultant's report. The Foundation officials reiterated their primary interest in the development of metropolitan community leadership and asked RPA to reconsider its proposal and attempt to incorporate more specific strategies for developing regional leadership. RPA was requested to submit an amended and revised proposal by the end of April.

The Ford Foundation officials were not asking RPA to generate an entirely new set of commitments and programs in a three-week period. They were asking RPA, after years of gestation, to reassert a commitment to broad civic leadership and devise a program to institutionalize this commitment.

RPA's leaders—Bradford, Norton, and Keith—spent much time over the next two weeks conferring with Foundation staff members, planners, political scientists, officers of other civic groups, and others. From the outset it was assumed, along the lines suggested in the consultant's report, that the organization of regional leadership would take place through the creation of a series of committees composed of "primary decision-makers" and experts. Many questions presented themselves. Should the committees be organized geographically or functionally? Or according to some compromise formula involving both bases? What kind of staff should be attached to these committees? What would the role of the staff be? What would the committees be expected to do? What end product was foreseen?

COMMITTEE BASES

In the consultation process, most of those whose opinions were asked recommended functional rather than geographically defined committees. One of RPA's primary commitments was to a regional focus of interest. The integrity of this commitment probably required a committee structure that would keep the regional focus paramount. A geographical breakdown of committees would have fractionalizing effects. Some qualified this conclusion by recognizing that in many sectors of the region key development problems were less than regional in scope. Further, since the region encompassed parts of three states, three different patterns of governmental structure and tax policies prevailed. Some subdivisions of the region, such as the nine northern New Jersey counties, were themselves as large as most metropolitan regions in the United States. There were, therefore, certain practical limitations to functionally defined committees.

A further argument for functionally defined committees was that these would parallel the committee structure of the Metropolitan Regional Council and thus facilitate a close working relationship.

RPA's leaders finally decided on a functional pattern. Aware of the complexities of organizing leadership in such a large region, they added the qualification that the several regional policy committees might form geographically defined subcommittees. After several committees had been thus divided, an "area development council" might be formed to coordinate the efforts of the various subcommittees in any one area of the region. Although this pattern would complicate the organizational pattern, it comprised the divergent views on the matter.

What particular functions would be appropriate bases for committee organization? The need to maintain flexibility and to channel RPA's limited resources into attacks on the most pressing problem led RPA to shy away from an adherence to any particular set of committees. RPA proposed rather that, when the development committee phase was to begin, the first group to be called into being would be a programming committee which would recommend what committees should be set up and in what order of priority. The proposal lists nine examples of policy area that might be considered: overall regional growth, transportation, redevelopment of obsolescent areas, new development, open space and recreation, regional immigrants, research and education, metropolitan governmental relations, and the relation of region to the nation.[16] The need for a staged approach, geared to the pressures of the moment, was recognized and explicit commitment deferred.

This postponement of an explicit decision may have avoided possible friction between RPA and the Ford Foundation. Such a list of committees would, in effect, be a statement of RPA's main interests. RPA's list and its priorities among the subjects on the list might have differed from the concerns and priorities the Foundation might have wished RPA to accept. Agreement might be easier to obtain when the time to set up committees actually came.

STAFF

All those consulted recognized the great importance of the quality and type of staff services provided. Some warned of the dangers of the committees being dominated by staff members promoting pet projects. One civic leader reported that his organization operated on the principle "that the staff is seen and not heard." Thus, there was recognition both of the crucial role of good staffwork and of the danger of committees becoming staff-run. Keith suggested resolving the dilemma by providing two types of staff persons: an "agenda-drafter" and a specialized research technician.[17] The "agenda-drafter" would presumably be a policy-oriented generalist capable of defining and explaining policy choices and acting as liaison between the committees and the technicians serving them.

COMMITTEE ROLE

RPA and Ford Foundation officials agreed that the first important product of the committees would be "white papers," setting forth the specific policy views of the groups. The committees should begin by drawing out of the Harvard study and supplementary research the policy implications of the findings and should then determine how to alter the projections of the study. The resulting policy papers were not regarded as the final goal of the committees—that goal was action to implement these policies. Policy statements were to be used as devices for mobilizing leadership resources to get the policies implemented.[18] Thus, policy development and leadership organization would go hand in hand.

RPA'S PROGRAM

During April, 1960, an ambitious proposal for organizing regional leadership was developed. It was enthusiastically endorsed by the RPA board and was submitted to the Ford Foundation on May 4, 1960. Echoing Norton's earlier statement about the primacy of leadership, this proposal goes further and makes clear RPA's commitment to the development of new policies through a "time-tested democratic process." The ambiguity in the 1958 proposal was finally and definitely resolved:

Much more is needed, however, than research, analysis and public information which RPA has brought to bear heretofore. We need new regional development objectives—and programs to carry such objectives out—evolved and supported by the region's leading citizens.[19]

The proposal contained a more elaborate analysis of "regional leadership" than any previous RPA statements. It was noted that the organization of regional leadership in the New York area presents serious problems not present to nearly the same degree elsewhere. Pittsburgh, for example, was mentioned as an instance of effective organization of "top leadership":

The New York region by comparison is about twice the area of Metropolitan Pittsburgh, with six times its population. . . . Indeed, Greater Newark . . . has half again as many people as the city of Pittsburgh. It is often said that it is possible to "get the leadership of Pittsburgh together in one room." The scale of the New York region is obviously of a different order.[20]

The proposal distinguished two levels of leadership. The "top leadership" level is made up of two types: the region's "national leadership" and its "regional leadership." The "national leaders" are

top leadership of the region's major [nationwide] institutions. . . . This group is principally concerned both in their business and their civic interest with, national and international affairs. Because they —and an important group of their employees—live and work in the New York region and because of the importance of this region as a national and international headquarters center, these resident "national leaders" have an interest in broad policy formulation for the region.[21]

The Harvard study's identification of New York's prominence as the nation's "headquarters town" only underscored the oft-expressed belief of RPA leaders that this national leadership, more than the leaders in any other metropolitan area, simply had too many national and global concerns to be attracted to organizations like RPA. However,

One of the principal services of the Harvard Study has been to re-awaken interest of the region's resident "national leadership" to a degree only comparable to the days of the preparation of the 1929 Plan. . . . Their increasing involvement with the objectives of the Association holds the prospects for major accomplishment.[22]

The other "top leadership group" is composed of men who

because of the nature of their work or its location, are generally focused on either the problems of a major sub-area of the region or on one function of regional development. They are, however, regional leaders because they are of sufficient stature to appreciate the regional context in which they operate. Examples of this "regional leadership" are top officers of organizations operating in and employing personnel from several counties of the region, or possibly department heads of national companies.[23]

The "second level of leadership" below these national and regional leaders

consists of the technical and professional people who represent the skilled manpower in the various disciplines concerned with metropolitan development. These technical advisors are to be found in universities, in business and labor organizations, government and civic agencies, and in the independent professions.[24]

This analysis of leadership concludes with the admission that this categorization is obviously oversimplified and imprecise but that "recognition of different levels of leadership is essential as the basis for an effective organizational structure through which leadership can act." [25]

Recognizing that its proposed program involved much more than research and study, RPA indicated that members of the various development committees would be "drawn from the groups described as resident 'national' and 'regional' leaders." [26] The programming committee, which would set the project in motion, might set up a technical advisory committee "consisting of selected top technical advisors and members of the permanent RPA staff." [27] The technical-professional level of leadership was to be used primarily in an advisory capacity. The RPA leaders were taking precautions against another subordination of leadership to research.

Turning to staff requirements for the development committees, the need for outside consultants and for improvement of RPA staff is noted, and a regional data center is recommended. Proposals for some sort of data center has been made for some time. At one point, RPA and the Port Authority jointly almost created one, and this was an important part of almost every proposal drafted by Henry Fagin.

RPA believed that eight to ten years could be expected to elapse between the beginning of the program and concrete actions to implement the recommended policies. It was estimated that the preparation of "white papers" would take about three years, that three more years would be required to "create regional awareness," and that two or three years later some results should begin to appear. RPA would need, over this ten-year period, foundation financing to the extent of about $2.7 million. It expected to raise an additional $1.7 million from nonfoundation sources at the same time. Consultation with Ford Foundation officials indicated a reluctance on the Foundation's part to give more than a three-year commitment, although the possibility of further support beyond three years was not foreclosed.

This was a most ambitious request. Previously, Foundation officials had urged RPA to "think bigger." This time RPA vigorously responded. The Ford Foundation rewarded this response in the summer of 1960 by making a grant of $400,000 to RPA to be expended over a three-year period. In making this grant, the Foundation underscored its primary interest in the organization of regional leadership. RPA was advised that because other foundations were likely to make grants for RPA's projections project, it was the Ford Foundation's hope that no more than $75,000 of the Ford grant would be used for that purpose. Also, the proposals for an area development committee and for a regional data center were excluded from the scope of the grant.

The emphasis of the grant was on developing regional leadership. Pleased with RPA's broadening interests and its greater attention to status and leadership, the Foundation called on RPA to try to recruit top-level community and educational leadership as its membership base and to experiment with the development of processes by which regional problems and policies could be effectively considered jointly by technical experts and top community figures.

Thus ended twenty years of search and trial. RPA had finally managed to restructure its commitments, devise a new program, and secure funds to implement its new course. The stability of these new commitments would depend, however, on how successfully they were institutionalized in the structure and policies of the organization and implemented in its day-to-day operations.

CHAPTER VII

The Implementation of Purpose

The turning point reached by RPA in 1960 was not a sudden development; a change in organizational commitment requires other organizational changes to be effective. Some of these changes had been taking place, facilitating RPA's choice of a new direction.

Personnel

Important changes in commitment are often accompanied by substantial shifts of personnel.[1] RPA experienced one of its greatest turnovers of personnel just prior to its formal change of direction in 1960. These personnel changes were both the cause and the consequence of RPA's shifting role and were reflected in the composition of both board and staff.

BOARD OF DIRECTORS

The RPA board experienced the largest turnover from 1957 to 1960 that it had ever had in any four-year period since RPA's inception. Twenty-four new members were added to the Board. Figures on additions to the Board for earlier four-year periods indicate the greater change experienced in the late 1950s (Table 5).[2] The additions to the board from 1957 to 1960 were thus about double the usual turnover for previous four-year periods.

THE IMPLEMENTATION OF PURPOSE

The new board members formed a well-balanced, prestigious group that broadened the range of interests represented on the RPA board. The group included three architects, a construction executive, and two utility vice-presidents—these represented no departure from the existing selection pattern. In addition, however, were RPA's next two presidents, Amory Bradford of the New York *Times* and James Schoff, president of Bloomingdale Bros.; William S. Renchard, president of the Chemical Bank New York Trust Company, RPA's first board

TABLE 5

NEW DIRECTORS ADDED TO THE BOARD OF THE REGIONAL PLAN ASSOCIATION, 1933–60

Dates	Number of Directors
1933–36	7
1937–40	12
1941–44	13
1945–48	12
1949–52	9
1953–56	11
1957–60	24

member from among the presidents of major commercial banks in New York since the 1930s; Cesar Bertheau, head of the People's Trust Company of Bergen County in Hackensack, New Jersey; Ralph Paine, publisher of *Fortune* and *Architectural Forum;* Arthur Langlie, ex-governor of the state of Washington and president of the McCall Corporation; Albert Merck, an investment executive; Harry Van Arsdale, head of the New York City Central Labor Council, RPA's first labor representative; two educators, Edwin Burdell, president of Cooper Union, and Wallace Sayre, professor of public administration at Columbia and chairman of RPA's committee on the future of the metropolitan regional council; David Yunich, then president of Bamberger's, R. H. Macy's New Jersey subsidiary, and now president of Macy's New York; market researcher Elmo Roper, another distinctly new type of board member; and others.

Luther Gulick, president of the Institute of Public Administration and formerly City Administrator of New York City, who came on the RPA board in 1956, was the first of this new breed. The board's nominating committee, which recruited most of these new directors, was headed each year by Otto Nelson and usually included Gulick, Willard Hampton of the New York Telephone Company, and Amory Bradford in 1959 and 1960.

These changes made RPA's board more representative and raised its status. This largely reconstituted board contained much new blood not strongly committed to RPA's habitual ways of viewing itself. Some of the new members had been on the advisory committee to the Harvard study; others were aware of the study and its import and were attracted to RPA by it. Most of them came to RPA at least mildly predisposed to favor resurrection of RPA's leadership commitments.

STAFF CHANGES

The board of directors did not initiate RPA's new program. A few directors joined Bradford and the leaders of the RPA staff in developing the new policies. The policy-forming initiative was at all times in the hands of this small group and, more specifically in the hands of the directors of the RPA staff, McKim Norton and John Keith.

Keith replaced Henry Fagin as executive director of RPA in mid-1959. Keith was the first nontechnician to occupy the post of director of the RPA staff. Holding a doctorate from the Institute of Public Administration, Keith had substantial experience in governmental research and had been associated with the American Society for Public Administration. He was selected in part precisely because his professional skills were administrative rather than technical. This shift in competence at the head of the staff was a recognition of the new demands being made on RPA and was designed to facilitate policy change.

Following RPA's development of a new program in 1960, Keith and Norton brought about other staff changes. Two economists were added to the staff. RPA had never employed an economist on a permanent basis before.

The other important staff change was the creation of the post of information director. In the 1930s RPA had had a small promotional staff whose time was largely devoted to promoting organization of official planning boards; these activities were discontinued in 1942. The office of public relations director was revived very briefly later but was eliminated in the 1949 belt-tightening. In contrast to the 1930s, when the field secretary was a salesman of planning ideology and generally subordinate to the technical staff, RPA now brought in another nontechnician and placed him on an equal level with the planning director.

William Shore, formerly editor of the *Public Administration Review,* came to RPA from a background of political science and public administration and had been associated with Keith. Shore's functions have been broadly interpreted, and he carries major responsibility for certain aspects of RPA's development committee program. The very existence of Shore's position stems from RPA's new commitments.

RPA's decision-making staff group includes Norton, Keith, Shore, and planning director Stanley Tankel. Others may be involved from time to time on particular issues, but these constitute the policy-forming core of the staff. This leadership core represents substantial resources of diverse skills and is probably the strongest staff-based leadership resource that RPA has ever possessed. This group strikes a balance between technical and broader administrative viewpoints and between commitment to new goals and continuity with the Association's past.

THE NEW JERSEY COMMITTEE

A major addition to RPA's operations came in 1960 with the establishment of a New Jersey committee of RPA, staffed by a well-known New Jersey planner, with a branch office in Newark. This was the culmination of much deliberation over how to keep a representative group of New Jersey leaders integrated into RPA's work.[3]

From the beginning, there had been a recognition that the nine northern New Jersey counties formed a subregion that, for some purposes, had to be considered independently of the rest of the region. Although there was substantial involvement of prominent New Jersey figures in the making of the Regional Plan and the early efforts of RPA, this involvement lapsed during the middle 1930s. McAneny had tried to build up RPA's support in New Jersey by creating a New Jersey committee in 1936–37. RPA could not generate enough interest to keep this group alive, and it soon lapsed. In the 1950s several planning issues came to a head in New Jersey, including the Meadowlands development and commuter railroad financing. There was a proposal for a $3-million northeastern New Jersey traffic study and growing manifestations of separatist tendencies among New Jersey figures. Consequently, RPA, eyeing a broadened leadership role, moved in to establish a New Jersey committee.

The committee is headed by George F. Smith, president of Johnson and Johnson and a member of RPA's Executive Committee. Nine members of the thirty-four-member committee are RPA board members. Ernest Erber, an experienced planner well known in New Jersey, serves as staff with the title New Jersey areas director.

RPA has also held two New Jersey conferences, to which about 200 business, civic, educational, labor, and other leaders have been invited. At the first of these, in 1961, an all-day discussion of the Harvard study and its implications was conducted. At the second, in 1963, policy recommendations of the

RPA New Jersey committee were discussed in detail. The committee is thus attempting to reach a broadly representative New Jersey audience and has become increasingly active in public policy issues at the state level. According to its staff director, the committee has been involved in the creation of a state-appointed Meadowlands Commission, drafting of middle-income housing legislation, promoting an interstate transportation compact, revising county planning powers, and acquiring recreation sites. RPA is thus developing a substructure to help effectuate its leadership commitments in an area where it has previously had some difficulty in maintaining strong support.

Program

The first order of business in RPA's new program was the projections project, designed to spell out the implications of the Harvard study in terms of land uses and capital costs. Because the study, as it stood, was not regarded as a suitable framework for RPA's next steps, it was understood by the Ford Foundation and the RPA leaders that this project would be started first, with the development committee operation gradually phased into the latter stages of the research.

The projections project was a substantial research effort. It involved the testing and modification of some of the Harvard hypotheses in the light of the 1960 census figures, the making of several studies, particularly of transportation, that were needed to fill gaps in the Harvard research, and finally the determination of what the study and subsequent research implied in terms of land uses and capital costs. The end product of this was the publication in September, 1962, of an RPA research bulletin, *Spread City*, widely regarded as one of RPA's best research reports.

Spread City[4] forecasts a population increase of 6 million by 1985 over the region's 1960 population. It anticipates that some

areas, such as Suffolk and Putnam Counties in New York and
Monmouth and Morris Counties in New Jersey, will treble in
population. The core area (defined as Manhattan, the Bronx,
Brooklyn, Queens, Hudson County, and Newark), however,
will decrease by 450,000. The character of this decline of the
core area is indicated by a net loss of 210,000 between 1950 and
1960. During the 1950s the core area experienced a gain of
821,000 Negroes and Puerto Ricans, which was more than offset by a loss of 1,031,000 non-Puerto Rican whites.

This outward movement of population and rapid development of the counties outside the core area will bring a spreading of population farther from jobs, which are anticipated to
remain relatively concentrated in the centers. The Harvard
study had indicated New York's importance as a "headquarters
town." Some crucial economic functions of New York involve
bringing large numbers of highly specialized people together
in varying relationships. Because of this situation, the economy
of the region will continue to be tied to the central core areas
despite the outward movement of population.

This increasing distance from home to job will be greatly
accentuated by suburban zoning policies. Regulations of 509
of the 551 municipalities in the region require, on the average,
the use of one-half acre of vacant land for a one-family house.
Thus, a net acre in these areas would provide for only $1\frac{1}{2}$
households, compared with 7 per net acre when Levittown was
built in the late 1940s and 10 to 50 dwellings produced by two-
family houses and garden apartments. These low-density zoning
regulations in large parts of the region will force many middle-
income families to build homes in the present fringe areas on
the outskirts of the region. Zoning makes the "spread city"
spread even more rapidly.

This spreading of population and increase of distance from
home to work will produce increasingly severe transportation
crises. Because of the lack of an efficient regional system of
mass transit, primary reliance will continue to be on the auto-

mobile. While a 37 percent increase in population between 1960 and 1985 is anticipated, a 73 percent increase in automobiles is expected.

The capital costs of the 100-mile spread city are estimated at $175 billion in public and private spending between 1960 and 1985. Operating costs of local government are expected to increase from $4.1 billion in 1957 to $8.4 billion in 1985.

In terms of livability, the spread city "would give most of us neither the benefits of the city nor the pleasures of the countryside." There will be poorer access to and hence less choice of "jobs, friends, recreation, goods, services, types of housing, and modes of travel."

Spread City is one of the most convincing, graphic, and well-researched forecasts of chaos that RPA has published. It constitutes RPA's point of departure for the development of specific policy proposals. While it is concerned with traditional planning matters such as land use, zoning, and transportation, it also points up "the social and moral questions raised by the abandonment of the cities to the disinherited," problems RPA had usually not explicitly dealt with in the past.

DEVELOPMENT COMMITTEE PROGRAM

While this work was going on, steps in the creation of development committees took place. These first steps were directed toward responses from the business and educational communities.

In February, 1961, and again a year later, four-day seminars were held at Arden House, in Harriman, New York, for groups of business executives from many of the region's major corporations. These conferences were designed to gauge the reactions of a selected group of business executives to RPA's program and to identify possible development committee members. Over 100 executives attended one or the other of these two seminars and were introduced to major policy implications of the Harvard study and the projections research. The executives invited were a careful blend of a few RPA board members, executives from some of RPA's contributors who were not represented on the board, and a number of others who had no previous connection with RPA.

The presentations stressed especially the implications of present development trends for the economic efficiency of the region—essentially an enlightened self-interest theme. The reports of the participants in the first Arden House conference were centered around deficiencies revealed by "looking at the region as though it were a production plant in competition with newer regions both at home and abroad." Off-the-record evaluations by RPA staff and board members of the reactions of individual participants in these conferences indicated that almost all were genuinely interested in RPA's efforts and might be brought into various development committees later.

Initial steps in the actual organization of a development committee were taken in setting up the nucleus of a committee on urban research and education in 1961. The issues and problems in this area could, RPA believed, "be isolated from the general background research of the projections project," [5] and this committee could therefore be set up first. A grant from the Lavanburg Foundation assisted in establishing this group. A nucleus of RPA board members and members of the Lavanburg Foundation board were selected as the initial members, and eventual addition of several university officials and other interested persons was anticipated.

The staff attached to the committee has to date produced eighteen working papers, the most important of which is an analysis prepared by one of RPA's new staff economists, of the uses and requirements for a regional data center. An RPA staff member has stated that, although RPA has proposed such a center many times, a really sophisticated and knowledgeable analysis of precisely what data should be collected, why, and how it would be utilized had never before been prepared. RPA now had its first really viable proposal for a continuing series of "Economic Reports on the State of the Region."

THE GOALS FOR THE REGION PROJECT

The next research step beyond the projections project is to be preparation of analyses of alternative patterns of development that the region might choose. As this report is in preparation, RPA, led by its new information director, has embarked on a major program of public education and mobilization of a broader base of support for RPA. Although *Spread City* received excellent press coverage, RPA felt that a wider exposure was necessary. Also, the report of the advisory committee to the Harvard study had recommended that RPA move into the previously neglected area of defining regional goals by identifying the values to be served by new development policies. Both citizen education and the need for a broad feedback of public reaction were stimuli for the RPA regional goals project.

RPA put on a series of five television programs during April and May of 1963. Prior to these, a large number of study groups were organized with the help of a variety of civic, professional, social, church, labor, and other groups. Background material and questionnaires were distributed in advance of the programs. The various study groups met, watched the RPA programs, discussed the issues raised, and filled out the questionnaires. The project was designed to give RPA detailed information about the preferences and tastes of the interested citizens of the region.

Over 600 study groups were organized, and 5,600 persons participated. "This appears to be the first time a planning organization has made a systematic effort on this scale, first to make clear what the realistic choices of living patterns are and then to find out the kind of pattern people want," McKim Norton stated.[6]

RPA also viewed the study-group program as absolutely essential to a democratic planning process:

It is difficult to assure that any political decision is truly representative of a constituency, but particularly is this true of planning decisions. The variety and scope of the differences in viewpoint and values on planning issues are far greater than on most, and they follow no general continuum, for example from liberal to conservative as in many economic issues. . . .

Typical party organizations . . . cannot represent a clear general point of view on these issues; the questions don't fall into a syndrome that suggests to the voter at election time, in a general way, how a candidate will stand on planning issues.

At the same time, these issues can, far more than most, be put into value terms. The elements in the decisions on which the citizen is expert can quite readily be isolated from the technical decisions for which we must rely on experts. What we need is a system for putting these value questions to citizens in a way which they can handle and getting from them responses that can be injected into the planning process. Regional Plan Association is trying to do this in a large-scale study group program.[7]

After the results of the study-group project are analyzed and digested, RPA will then move to the final stage, the actual selection of the development committees. The contacts generated through all these efforts to gain public understanding and support will be exploited in recruiting development committee members. The establishment of these committees is planned for mid-1964.

RPA is thus making an intensive effort to follow through the new program of leadership undertaken in 1960. Its operations are no longer confined to narrowly physical features; broad economic and social issues are equally important. The functions and limits of technical expertise are better understood, there is better understanding of the limits of the self-executing-plan philosophy, and a great deal more than lip service is being paid to the ideals of democratic participation in the planning process. RPA is, in many ways, a new organization since 1960.

Finances

In earlier times, RPA's survival was jeopardized by a lack of mission and by dwindling financial support. Although RPA managed to devise a new program with foundation support, the financial problem remained. RPA's new plan of operation is more costly than its earlier activities. The long-term success of RPA's endeavors depends on finding enough new support to take up the slack that will be left when foundation support expires. RPA estimates that it must have an annual budget of at least $300,000 to carry out its program commitments. Without foundation support, these funds would have to come mainly from corporate subscriptions.

How ambitious this goal is can be seen from the record of RPA's corporate support. In 1949, the first year after the withdrawal of Russell Sage support, RPA's corporate subscriptions amounted to about $40,000; by 1957, when important organizational changes began to take place, support had gradually risen to just under $50,000. Increases then came more rapidly; subscriptions were up to $75,000 by 1960 and to almost $100,000 in 1962 (Tables 6 and 7). Impressive as this is, it is

TABLE 6

REGIONAL PLAN ASSOCIATION INCOME, 1951–62

Year	Membership Dues	Corporate Subscriptions	Foundations, Special Studies, and Miscellaneous	Total
1951	$ 3,710	$45,495	$ 4,705	$ 53,910
1952	6,135 *	43,015	11,878	61,028
1953	8,193	43,269	15,659	67,121
1954	8,563	49,862	7,482	65,907
1955	11,273	49,240	31,709	92,222
1956	11,093	47,760	152,814 †	211,667
1957	12,284	49,915	206,364	268,563
1958	14,843 *	55,391	266,115	336,349
1959	14,800	74,450	91,300	180,550
1960 ‡	$ 82,741 ¶		87,612	170,353
1961	105,002 ¶		170,287	275,289
1962	20,545	98,160	196,714	315,419

* Dues increased.
† Metropolitan regional project began.
‡ Eight-month fiscal year because of shift of Association fiscal-year dates.
¶ Available records do not distinguish membership dues and corporate subscriptions for 1960 and 1961.

TABLE 7

REGIONAL PLAN ASSOCIATION
NONFOUNDATION INCOME, 1962

Contribution	Number	Amount	Average
Membership dues:			
Personal	331	$ 4,890	
Nonprofit organizations	208	3,182	
Organizations	75	3,545	
Municipal	138	8,928	
Total	752	$20,545	
Corporate subscriptions:			
Under $1,000	82	$26,310	$ 321
$1,000 or more	32	71,850	2,245
Total	114	$98,160	$ 861

far short of the projected goal. Despite RPA's constant financial plight, little systematic solicitation was undertaken until very recently. A membership secretary, whose responsibilities include preparation of materials necessary for solicitation campaigns, has been added to the staff.

With the increase in RPA's corporate income, gradual changes in the pattern of its contributions have taken place. Today, as always, the utilities, banks, and insurance companies form the core of RPA's support (Table 8). These firms' contributions, however, are declining as a percentage of the total RPA corporate support. From 1941 to 1944 these three groups constituted 100 percent of RPA's corporate support, by 1952–53 their share had declined to about 80 percent, and in 1962, it was just over 60 percent. Among these three groups, the utilities have always been the leading contributor. Their share of the 1962 corporate contribution to RPA was almost 30 percent. Until very recently, insurance companies ranked second and banks third. Among the banks, 75 to 80 percent of contributions formerly came from savings banks; now savings banks and commercial banks are virtually equal in their support of RPA. Commercial banks have thus been an important source of RPA's increment in income.

RPA has traditionally been very weak among manufacturing concerns. For some time there were no contributions from this source at all. In 1952, industry constituted barely 4 percent of RPA's corporate support; this was up to 18 percent in 1962.

TABLE 8

BREAKDOWN OF RPA CORPORATE SUBSCRIPTIONS, 1962

Category	Number of Subscribers	Amount	Percentage of Total Corporate Subscriptions
Utilities	11	$27,800	28.3
Manufacturers	22	17,950	18.2
Commercial banks	14	10,650	10.8
Savings banks	24	9,800	10.0
Life insurance companies	5	9,500	9.7
Retailers	5	5,000	5.2
Publishing	4	3,500	3.6
Investment bankers and trusts	5	2,750	2.8
Food	5	1,400	1.4
Savings and loan associations	10	860	0.9
Transportation	2	700	0.7
Advertising agencies	1	500	0.5
Miscellaneous	6	7,750	7.9
Total	114	$98,160	100.0

In that year 22 manufacturing firms contributed a total of $17,950 to RPA. Only two of these contributions exceeded $1,000. Industry appears to be the major untapped source of revenue for RPA.

RPA, having blocked out a new program, continues to face the task of creating an expanded financial base to support that program on a permanent basis. Once again, RPA's leaders, this time assisted by professional consultants, mulled over the question of how it could sell itself to potential supporters, particularly among the industrial companies. One of RPA's leaders remarked, "The more things change, the more they remain the same. We've got a new program, but the long-term financial picture isn't much better than it has been. Money is still the number one problem."

This financial imperative might, over time, produce some alteration of RPA's commitments. This could occur by distortion of commitments to meet the requirements of fund-raising (if, for example, RPA expanded its direct services to business to the detriment of its other activities), or it could occur by RPA's explicitly choosing to reduce or eliminate some parts of the program because of inadequate financial support. Further foundation support beyond 1963 could alleviate the time pressure of the financial situation and prevent this from seriously distorting RPA's commitments, at least in the short run. An expanded leadership role requires an expanded financial base.

Public Policy for the Region: RPA and Government

The major thrust of RPA's revitalized commitment to regional leadership in public policy was not scheduled until the alternatives project was completed and a system of development committees established. In view of its new program, new leadership, enhanced prestige, and recent publicity in connection with the Harvard study, RPA was not inclined to stay completely out of public policy questions pending completion of the scheduled studies.

Within the region, RPA has continued to enjoy cordial relations with the Port of New York Authority. RPA has supported the Port Authority's proposals for a World Trade Center, its assumption of operating control of the tubes of the bankrupt Hudson and Manhattan railroad, now Port Authority Trans-Hudson (PATH), and strongly supported the Port Authority when it was under investigation by the House Judiciary Committee.

The Metropolitan Regional Council has not fared as well as RPA had hoped.[8] Although internally divided on whether it should seek official status, MRC secured passage of appropriate interlocal agreement legislation in the three states. This legislation was permissive, allowing local governments to enter into agreements with each other interstate. An insufficient number of local councils adopted MRC's interlocal agreement, however, and, under severe pressures, MRC finally in 1964 gave up its efforts to obtain official status. It decided to reconstitute itself as a voluntary organization of public officials rather than as an association of communities. Under this arrangement, officials will participate as individuals rather than as representatives of local governments, and the Council will be limited to study and advisory functions.

Despite the substantial political opposition the Council encountered, it has nevertheless managed to stay in existence. This fact may attest to an awareness of regional problems and the dimensions of their solution by many of the member officials, even though these concerns may not be widely shared by their constituents. If so, a Council revitalized along the lines suggested by RPA's Sayre Committee may yet develop.

Since 1952 RPA has repeatedly called for the establishment of a tri-state agency to make a comprehensive survey of regional transportation needs. Although RPA did not have a definite series of proposals for a regional transportation system, the intimate connection between the automobile and the spread-city pattern was obvious. RPA frequently called on the states to provide some kind of aid to the sagging commuter railroads until some more adequate comprehensive solution was developed. In 1959 RPA's transportation committee, headed by Walter Binger, issued a strong recommendation to the state governments calling for an official tri-state metropolitan transportation commission.[9] This commission should develop a long-range transportation plan and generate support for putting it into effect. A tri-state transportation committee was established by agreement of the three governors in 1961, and RPA has provided technical advice and assistance to it since its inception.

This committee, which RPA regards as a most significant and encouraging development, is now seeking legal status through interstate compact.

RPA has moved beyond its recommendation for an official regional transportation study and has called for

the establishment of a public regional transportation agency empowered to contract for or otherwise insure rail commuter operations within the metropolitan region. Such an action agency could be the recipient of public funds appropriated to insure essential commuter rail service in the public interest.[10]

RPA thus continues to prod the state governments to assume responsibility for devising and implementing a regional transportation policy. An increasingly important aspect of RPA's program is serving as supporter and critic of state and regional agencies as these agencies gradually begin to assume some responsibility for regional problems.

Finally, the crucial leverage needed to produce regionwide planning and policy development may come, as in the 1930s, from Washington. Several senators and representatives from the region have become interested in regional problems, especially transportation. Late in 1960 RPA was commissioned by the Senate Committee on Interstate and Foreign Commerce to produce a pilot study on commuter transportation in the New York region.[11] Since 1961 legislation has been introduced each year for federal grants and loans to state and local agencies for improving commuter transportation, providing those agencies are operating within the framework of a comprehensive metropolitan transportation plan.

Walter Binger and Stanley Tankel appeared before the Subcommittee on Housing of the Senate Banking and Currency Committee in 1962 urging the adoption of the administration-backed transportation legislation. An RPA memorandum noted that these proposals would "organize the federal pitcher and call for the metropolitan area catcher." [12] RPA's only reservation was that the proposed legislation would authorize appropriations of only $500 million over three fiscal years. Binger stated that the New York region alone needed about half the total appropriation the bill would authorize.[13]

The Federal Housing Act of 1961 also contains provisions for federal aid for the acquisition and development of open space and recreation areas, provided regional planning requirements are met. RPA submitted the Parks–Recreation–Open Space Study it had made jointly with the Metropolitan Regional Council to the Housing and Home Finance Agency. The HHFA decided that the RPA-MRC study met the planning requirements of the Act. RPA continued to be relied on by HHFA as the New York region's planning agency for about two years, until the Tri-State Transportation Committee, a public agency, began to develop a comprehensive planning program. During this period, twenty open-space programs were approved for the region, supported by federal grants of almost $2.8 million.

After 1964 regional transportation planning will be required to obtain federal highway funds for metropolitan area roads. Other proposals are pending which would extend the metropolitan planning requirement to other federal grant-in-aid programs. The potential federal stimulus to metropolitan planning in the 1960s and beyond seems far greater than that of the 1930s, when the planning requirement was attached mainly to public works projects and was tempered by the circumstances of a national emergency.

Thus, as the projections project and alternatives study were providing RPA with a new platform, the Association was also gaining—and cultivating—an audience. For the first time since the 1930s RPA seemed to be generating the commitments, policies, and audience that would enable it to function as a viable center of leadership for the metropolitan region. It appears that the commitments generated over the last several years have been successfully institutionalized, although the process of policy development and leadership recruitment is not yet complete. RPA is entering an era of great expectations unparalleled since 1929.

CHAPTER VIII

Summary and Conclusions

The basic purpose of organizing metropolitan community leadership is to establish a process for discovering and articulating the common interests of the region and for making and implementing public policies based on those interests more adequately than can be done in the absence of metropolitan organization. It is an effort to organize a nascent political process for the region. This is an extremely demanding task. The great size, diversity, and complexity of a large metropolitan area require more systematic attention to the organization of leadership than is the case with most civic groups, whose horizons are correlated with political boundaries. Ritualistic exhortation and warm-hearted zeal may suffice as a leadership role for some organizations; a regional association requires much more. These requirements include research for policy development and the organization of representative community interests, both to participate in defining policy goals and to promote the adoption of recommended policies.

The record of the RPA indicates the great difficulties of comprehending and implementing such a demanding and difficult task. Because of the vastly greater size of the New York region, RPA has faced tasks of a greater magnitude than organizations in other areas, although the basic problems are probably common to most large metropolitan areas.

At the outset, RPA lacked a clear conception of its role beyond the promotion of the Regional Plan, and there was some ambiguity about appropriate strategies for doing that. It has taken RPA, a pioneer in this field, decades to define and institutionalize the requirements of a regional leadership role. Its history is therefore important for an understanding of the dimensions of the problem of civic leadership in metropolitan areas.

RPA has always wanted to see its plans implemented, but the nature of its role in this connection has been problematic. From the beginning, the leadership role was largely separate from and subordinate to the making of the plans. In practice, this role was largely the promotion of official planning machinery. The subordinate character of the leadership role facilitated its later decline. Because the leadership role was not systematically conceived in the beginning, it was difficult to revive later.

When many of the proposals of the Regional Plan had been carried out and federal spending for public works declined, RPA was faced with the need to generate new policies. Unable to do this readily, it became increasingly cautious and withdrawn. The efforts of Norton, Windels, and Clark to redirect RPA in the 1940s did not produce a new role that could be readily implemented. Consequently, RPA's leadership role continued to languish. Concern for organizational maintenance predominated, and continued technical dominance of the organization was inevitable.

Efforts to renovate RPA's leadership role in the 1950s were more successful, culminating in the program developed in 1960. What were the circumstances and conditions that made the renaissance of RPA as a leadership institution more likely in the 1950s than in the 1940s?

Conditions of Organizational Revival

In the 1950s impetus for organizational change came both from internal concerns and from the external environment. The stimuli for innovation in the 1940s had been largely internal.

The minutes of RPA's board and its executive committee from 1940 onward are filled with numerous discussions of the

Association's future program. Despite these periodic recognitions of the need for innovation, no more than moderate efforts were made, as long as the stimulus was primarily from within. Not many proposals were developed that strayed very far from the Association's habitual commitments. Those that did go further were sometimes scaled down in practice. For example, the decision to undertake economic studies in the 1940s continuously had to be justified to the RPA board. In retrospect, almost all concerned acknowledge that the resources and staff devoted to these studies were not nearly adequate to produce the result that was intended. Internal demands for change were inadequate, by themselves, to accomplish major organizational innovations.

Another obstacle to the achievement of internally stimulated innovation was the lack of sufficient staff resources to permit the leaders of the staff to devote a significant proportion of their time to long-range organizational planning. As March and Simon indicate,[1] initiation of new program proposals is usually preceded by a period of search activity in which new alternatives are formulated and evaluated. Despite occasional internal demands for change, the group's top staff did not have time to become actively involved in the search processes likely to lead to important changes in organizational commitment. Under conditions of limited resources and constant time pressures, the attention of RPA's overworked top staff has usually been devoted to short-run problems and to the group's regular operating program.

Concern for organizational maintenance mitigates against planned innovation. It is only in highly exceptional circumstances that considerations of RPA's long-term role have been a top-priority concern of RPA's leadership. There are only three instances of such consideration: Norton's concern in the early 1940s when he became executive vice-president, the foundation-sponsored study of metropolitan organizations in other regions in 1957, and the efforts made early in 1960 with the help of an outside consultant to devise a new program that would respond to the challenge of the Advisory Committee report and secure foundation support. Only the first of these occasions was the result of primarily internal forces. Freedom of leaders to engage in long-range planning was rendered more important because of the initial ambiguity of RPA's role after the Regional Plan and official planning were largely established.

With such limited organizational resources to devote to long-range planning and the development of program alternatives, only a very considerable pressure could cause program revision to become a matter of high priority. Short of a most severe internal crisis, such pressures were far more likely to be generated by significant events and changes in the group's external environment.

At least three general conditions conducive to renovation of RPA's role were present in the late 1950s that were largely absent in the 1940s. First, large-scale foundation resources were available to help finance program development and organizational changes. RPA's leaders and the officials of Ford and other foundations were thinking along the same lines. Although RPA would almost certainly have chosen the same path under any circumstances, foundation interest hastened and stimulated RPA's development.

Second, the report of the Advisory Committee on the Harvard Study was a powerful challenge. With the imminent publication of the Study's findings and the strong desire of the Advisory Committee for an appropriate follow-up, long-range program change became a top priority for RPA's leadership. The result was approval of a specific new program by the board and its submission to the Ford Foundation within seven months of the advisory committee's report to the RPA board.

In addition to these external influences, a third factor not present earlier was operative. The changes on RPA's board and staff in the late 1950s were greater, both quantitatively and qualitatively, than in any other period of RPA's history. This new blood in RPA's leadership was able to capitalize on the Harvard Study and on the increasing concern of the business community and foundations and to help immeasurably in enabling RPA to respond favorably to its opportunities and challenges. A solid organizational base for developing and institutionalizing important changes was present for perhaps the first time.

Leadership and Research: A Balanced Conception

The program developed by RPA in 1960 put RPA's commitments to research and to the organization of regional leadership on a par for the first time. Indeed, the new program does not view them as separate functions but as integrated aspects of a carefully planned organizational strategy. RPA did not come by this balanced conception overnight. It developed out of years of experience in which RPA gradually came to appreciate fully the interdependence of research and leadership functions.

The committee on the regional plan separated the task of making plans from that of organizing support for carrying them out. There was little attempt made to involve representative community interests in the making of the Regional Plan. Although the leaders of the committee may have envisioned a potent leadership role, the organization of support turned out to be largely confined to promotion of official planning. Even this mild promotional role was drawn into question in the mid-1930s, when official planning was at least nominally established. Although the founders may not have clearly intended it, a technical predominance was built into RPA from the beginning. The circumstances produced by the federal public works programs of the 1930s enhanced these tendencies.

Competing with this technical orientation was a conception of leadership based on a board composed of the region's first citizens—persons who combined high social status, economic influence, and broad civic concern. The political skills of George McAneny, supported by some of these citizens, made RPA a significant force in regional development during the 1930s. Yet regional leaders were hard to find, and RPA's role was largely confined to public works, with the major stimulus coming from Washington. McAneny's conception of leadership was the subordinate theme in the RPA of the 1930s. Built-in tendencies toward technical dominance were reinforced by events and generally prevailed.

The decline of RPA's leadership role demonstrated that leadership on a regional scale must be more than an after-thought to research. It must provide for a continuous process of policy development. As the Regional Plan's projects were car-ried out, RPA lost its program. Promotion of public policy became little more than generalized exhortation in the ab-sence of specific policies to advocate. RPA tended to back away from new issues of public policy and to contract its leadership role. In the Stuyvesant Town incident, for example, RPA, without a definite position on publicly subsidized urban re-development, limited its involvement to a very general state-ment of principle.

Furthermore, the technical dominance that prevailed in the 1930s frustrated the systematic cultivation of a broad base of regionwide support. An effective two-way pattern of communi-cation between a good technical staff and broadly representa-tive community interests could provide citizen education on public issues and could feed informed community preferences into continuous research on regional development. Because such a base of support was not organized in the 1930s, there was no way except through research to maintain an on-going policy development process when the Regional Plan was used up. This was not a tenable alternative, since declining financial support made it impossible to maintain the research operations needed to generate new regional policies. Thus, a minimal

organization of support, involving at least the recruitment of
a solid financial base, was necessary even under the most extreme assumptions about the self-executing qualities of good
plans.

The close relationship of leadership and research for policy
development is also pointed up by the fact that, while a leadership role requires substantial political skills, the presence of
those skills is not a sufficient condition for a strong public
policy impact. All RPA's presidents have possessed notable administrative skills and political abilities. Paul Windels, for example, was a top political strategist of the La Guardia era, and
Harold Osborne, after retirement, became mayor of a suburban city deeply involved in urban renewal and redevelopment. Yet no president since McAneny has led the Association
to quite as great an impact on public policy, probably because
only McAneny was working from a well-researched, integrated
scheme of policies. Windels and Osborne both had to give top
priority to maintaining and developing RPA as an organization.

In the early 1950s questions of RPA's competence and status
became acute. Its debilitated financial condition and diminished staff could no longer meet important research needs
of RPA's constituency. The need for funds made improved
community status imperative. Further organizational decline
might force RPA out of existence. The ensuing proposal for
regional economic studies was designed to boost RPA's increasingly tepid research and service operations. It was not
necessarily designed to serve as a basis for important alterations
in RPA's commitments. Its ultimate result might be a new
regional plan, but at the beginning there was no indication that
research and leadership roles would be related much differently
than in the making of the Plan in the 1920s. Indeed, the events
of the 1950s indicate pressure within RPA to assimilate the
new studies and new experiences into the framework of traditional commitments. Only gradually did a new conception of

leadership emerge and then under the pressures of external events that RPA could not afford to ignore.

The program that finally resulted is substantially different in its conception of leadership from the program of the 1920s. In the development of the Regional Plan, a plan was made first; it was then promoted among the region's public authorities and leading citizens. In the present effort, RPA is making a systematic attempt to involve in the planning process a broad spectrum of representative community interests throughout the region, especially in the crucial stage of defining the goals and values to be embodied in a regional plan. To the extent that this strategy succeeds, RPA will be developing a democratic planning process for the region. RPA's research and planning functions become a basis for involving and organizing a broad regional leadership.

Research and planning seem to be a particularly appropriate focus for the development of metropolitan leadership. In the politically fragmented metropolitan area, no public agency is likely to plan or to collect a full range of balanced data on a regional basis. In a complex metropolitan region, substantial research data is needed before intelligent policy alternatives can be developed. This is not to suggest that the "facts" will yield a single obvious policy proposal; but a detailed knowledge of the region as it exists, knowledge not likely to be available anywhere else, is fundamental to effective planning. Thus, research and study will always be an important function of a regional citizens' group like RPA.

The task, however, is not merely one of discovering the region. It also involves, as an RPA leader expressed it, convincing key segments of the region's citizenry that they live in the region that RPA is discovering. Regional planning is still a substantial act of faith. Involvement of representative regional interests helps to educate them to the realities that are the region and, more importantly, feeds their preferences back into the planning process—preferences that are now based on information rather than ignorance. The research task must be undertaken in any event; it can be skillfully used as a tool of leadership and democratic participation in planning as well. It is likely that involvement of regional citizenry in a planning process will generate more lasting interest and support than a clarion call for metropolitan government or for any other single issue whose basis has not been solidly documented in a way that people can understand.

Regional consciousness is today greater than it was in the 1920s; it is, nevertheless, not rampant. RPA's experience clearly indicates that such a consciousness cannot be created overnight but has to be carefully stimulated over a period of time. RPA's present program is a careful, systematic beginning.

Toward a Metropolitan Polity

The successful exercise of RPA's leadership commitment depends upon the nature of the political environment in which the group seeks to act. RPA's leadership role is complicated considerably by the group's regional focus of interest. No governmental structure corresponding to the scope of RPA's interest exists. The problems of effective action at the regional level are such that they undoubtedly formed an additional reason for the earlier subordination and eclipse of RPA's leadership role.

If RPA's interests were confined to city planning, it could become part of the constituency of the several agencies of city government that controlled the policies in which RPA was interested. Initiative in developing policies would be shared with these public agencies and with other interest groups. It would not bear the great burdens of research and policy development that it now tries to assume. In a structured political environment, the tasks of cooperation with and criticism of relevant public agencies do not require either the research effort or the leadership effort that regionally oriented action requires.

RPA faces a political environment with a seemingly infinite number of decision points in the multiplicity of state, local, and federal authorities in the region. Some policies with which RPA may be concerned may not be explicitly made by anyone but result from an aggregation of decisions made by a multiplicity of agencies and individuals. The greatest single need for achieving RPA's long-termed objectives is some form of regional decision-making structure. RPA needs, in short, a metropolitan polity or some functional equivalent.

RPA is committed to planning within the framework of democratic processes. Securing a consensus of the community on the goals embodied in a plan is a vital part of RPA's present program. Such a consensus (or lack of it) is most naturally registered through political processes. If a metropolitan polity existed and was attempting to devise and implement regional development policies, considerable expressions of the sentiments of interested segments of the community would doubtless be elicited. In the absence of a metropolitan polity, RPA is seeking to construct a rough substitute in its study group and development committee programs.

This is an enormously complicated task. RPA hopes that it will be able to identify a relatively small number of key decisions that, while perhaps not effectuating its recommendations completely, might partially realize them and create choice situations where local governments would have more incentives to follow the plan than not. This identification requires of RPA both skilled technical research and sophisticated political analysis. The present program seeks not to rely too heavily on public education by itself but to influence a few key decisions that will result in a restructuring of the choices presented to local governments and key individuals. Furthermore, RPA's new policies are certain to be going against the tide of at least some existing preferences. Thus, while RPA deplores the spread city, this emerging pattern is the result of the interaction of many choices made by many individuals and agencies. Although no one has explicitly willed the spread city, many people are making choices that make the spread city inevitable. RPA is faced with the task of reinterpreting those choices in a broader regional context in hopes of altering them.

Despite these obstacles, RPA's program holds out the possibility of a new regional plan and the development of a more adequate power base. The present program is designed to broaden RPA's base of support and develop a more pluralistic, diversified constituency for RPA. The early conception of leadership built around "leading citizens" who constituted a patrician elite of social status and wealth was probably dated even at the time it was espoused. In any case, it is now recognized as being too simple a conception. While RPA continues to cultivate business support and to draw a broad spectrum of business executives and their staff aids into its program, it has substantially broadened its contacts with labor unions, church leaders, and educators. The study-group program and the development committee project together form probably the most extensive and systematic effort ever made to recruit some approximation of a genuine metropolitan community leadership.

This task of organizing metropolitan community leadership would proceed much more rapidly if some equivalent to a metropolitan polity appeared on the scene. Although general metropolitan government does not seem to be in the offing, there is a distinct possibility that the increasing insistence on regional planning requirements in federal grant-in-aid legislation will stimulate the development of some kind of regional decision-making process. Efforts are now being made to give the Tri-State Transportation Committee, established in 1961, official status as a regional planning agency. Such an agency, plus the relevant federal agencies that approve the plans on which applications for funds are based, would form, for some purposes, the equivalent of a metropolitan polity. Whether the present Tri-State Transportation Commission gets official status or not, continued federal planning stipulations in grant-in-aid legislation will force the development of some kind of machinery to comply with these requirements.

These developments provide RPA with a great opportunity and a great challenge. RPA would have a specific governmental target. As more regional research and planning was done by an official agency whose budget and staff were considerably larger than RPA's, RPA would not have the sole burden of doing regional research and could divert some of its resources into other activities.

The great challenge presented by such a development would be the challenge of democratic participation in the choice of planning goals. Lacking a regional governmental structure, a regional planning agency would probably be at best only in-directly responsible to the region's citizens, and final authority to give or withhold federal funds would lie in Washington.

For these reasons, a strong regional civic organization posses-sing some competence in the field of planning seems essential. The development of a broad base of support among the re-gion's citizens and organizations and the development of pro-cesses by which the preferences of these supporters can be regis-tered are consequently requirements of great importance for the future of RPA in the kind of political environment that seems to be evolving. Organizations like RPA will be of key importance in assuring broad public consideration of planning goals. Although research will continue to be an indispensable part of RPA's program, it is likely to become a more action-oriented group than it has been in the past. It is probably on the threshold of a regional political process.

RPA's ultimate purpose is the creation of an enhanced sense of community and of conditions under which individuals can enjoy a meaningful relationship to their environment. The development of both voluntary and governmental institutions focused on the metropolitan community is a vital step in this direction. RPA's reactivated commitment to regional leadership provides the best opportunity since the making of the Regional Plan to move toward these goals. If RPA enjoys any measure of success in its new program, the makers of the 1929 Plan will have built better than they knew. Long after the Plan has been forgotten, the association they formed to promote that Plan will be making a continuing contribution to the quest for community in the modern world.

Organizational Charts of the RPA

CHART 1. 1930–32

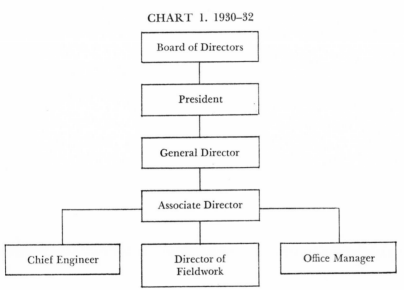

Also engineers, draftsmen, and clerical and office personnel.

CHART 2. 1932-33

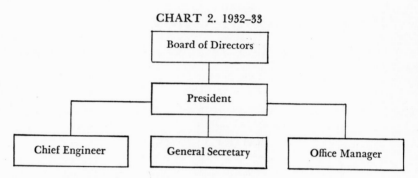

Also engineers, draftsmen, and clerical and office personnel.

CHART 3. 1933-37

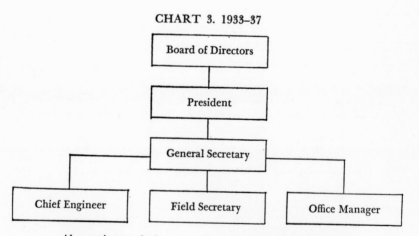

Also engineers, draftsmen, and clerical and office personnel.

CHART 4. 1937–40

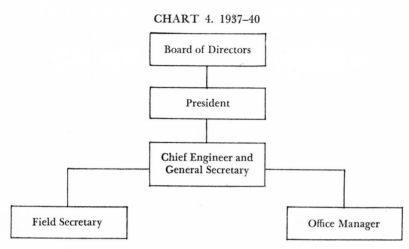

Also engineers, draftsmen, and clerical and office personnel.

CHART 5. 1940–42

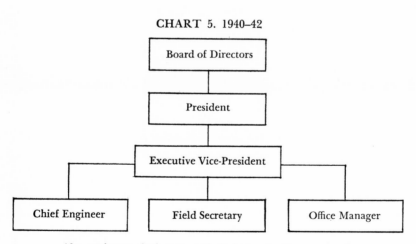

Also engineers, draftsmen, and clerical and office personnel.

CHART 6. 1942–58

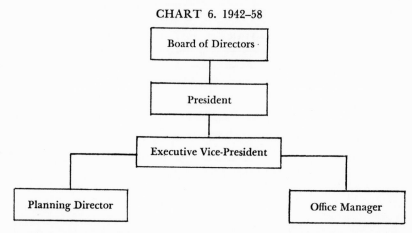

Also engineers, draftsmen, planners, and library, clerical, and office personnel.

CHART 7. 1958–61

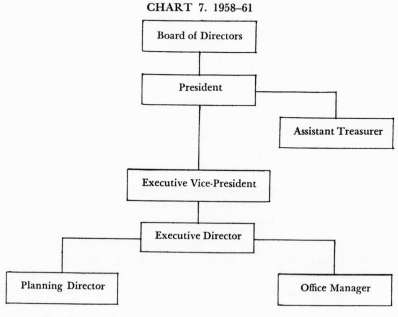

Also planners, draftsmen, and library, clerical, and office personnel.

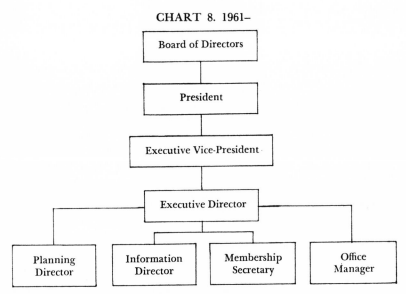

CHART 8. 1961–

Board of Directors

President

Executive Vice-President

Executive Director

Planning Director

Information Director

Membership Secretary

Office Manager

Also planners, economists, draftsmen, and library, clerical and office personnel.

Presidents and Staff Directors of RPA

RPA Presidents

1929–40   George McAneny (public official)
1940–42   Frederick C. Horner (corporate executive)
1942–52   Paul Windels (attorney)
1952–59   Harold S. Osborne (consulting engineer)
1959–62   Amory H. Bradford (newspaper executive)
1962–64   James S. Schoff (department store executive)
1964–   C. McKim Norton (attorney, planner)

RPA Staff Heads

1930–32   George B. Ford (Title: General Director.
          Training: Architecture)
1932–33   George McAneny, President of the Association
1933–37   Lawrence M. Orton (Title: General Secretary.
          Training: Planning)
1937–40   Harold M. Lewis (Title: Chief Engineer and
          General Secretary. Training: Civil Engineering)
1940–42   C. McKim Norton (Title: Executive Vice-President.
          Training: Law)
1942–52   C. McKim Norton, Executive Vice-President
          Frederick P. Clark (Title: Planning Director.
          Training: Architecture)
1952–58   C. McKim Norton, Executive Vice-President
          Henry Fagin, Planning Director
          (Training: Architecture)
1958–59   C. McKim Norton, Executive Vice-President
          Henry Fagin, Executive Director
          Douglas Powell, Planning Director
          (Training: Planning)

1959–60   C. McKim Norton, Executive Vice-President
           John P. Keith, Executive Director
              (Training: Administration)
           Douglas Powell, Planning Director
1960–64   C. McKim Norton, Executive Vice-President
           John P. Keith, Executive Director
           Stanley B. Tankel, Planning Director
              (Training: Planning)

Notes

Introduction

1. The metropolitan region is defined by the Regional Plan Association to include these counties: in New York, the five counties of New York City, plus Nassau, Suffolk, Westchester, Rockland, Orange, Putnam, and Dutchess; in New Jersey, Hudson, Essex, Union, Passaic, Bergen, Monmouth, Middlesex, Somerset, and Morris; in Connecticut, Fairfield (see map facing p. 1).

2. Robert C. Wood, *1400 Governments: The Political Economy of the New York Metropolitan Region* (Cambridge, Mass., Harvard University Press, 1961), p. 1.

3. Wallace S. Sayre and Herbert Kaufman, *Governing New York City: Politics in the Metropolis* (New York, Russell Sage Foundation, 1960).

Chapter I. Origins

1. See, e.g., David B. Truman, *The Governmental Process: Political Interests and Public Opinion* (New York, Knopf, 1951), pp. 112–15.

2. See Philip Selznick, *Leadership in Administration* (New York, Harper & Row, 1957), Chap. 2.

3. Quoted in a letter from Charles Dyer Norton to Frederick A. Delano, Nov. 24, 1921; and in John M. Glenn, L. Brandt, and F. Emerson Andrews, *Russell Sage Foundation* (New York, Russell Sage Foundation, 1947), II, 439.

4. The story of the Chicago Plan is told in Charles Moore, *Daniel H. Burnham: Architect, Planner of Cities* (Boston and New York, Houghton Mifflin, 1921), II, 14–15, 97–115, 171–72. The following discussion draws on Moore's account.

5. *Ibid.*, p. 112.   6. *Ibid.*, p. 98.

7. Letter from Norton to Delano, Nov. 24, 1921, p. 1. Correspondence of Norton and Delano and other papers relating to the Regional Plan were made available to the writer by C. McKim Norton, son of Charles Dyer Norton and president of the RPA.

8. Letter of W. H. Taft to New York *Times*, March 10, 1923.

9. Norton to Delano, Nov. 24, 1921, p. 3.

10. George McAneny, *Reminiscences* (New York, Columbia University Oral History Project, 1949), p. 34.

11. *Ibid.*, pp. 37–38.

12. Norton to Delano, Nov. 24, 1921, p. 5.

13. *Ibid.*   14. *Ibid.*, p. 6.   15. *Ibid.*, p. 7.

16. *Ibid.*, p. 8.   17. *Ibid.*, p. 9.

18. Quoted in *ibid.*   19. *Ibid.*, p. 12.

20. McAneny, *Reminiscences*, pp. 37–38.

21. Letter of Gift from Margaret Olivia Sage to Russell Sage Foundation Trustees, April 19, 1907. Reprinted in Glenn *et al.*, *Russell Sage Foundation*, pp. 667–68.

22. Norton to Delano, Nov. 24, 1921, p. 12.

23. *Ibid.*, p. 18; Glenn *et al.*, *Russell Sage Foundation*, p. 439.

24. *Ibid.*, pp. 439–40.   25. *Ibid.*, p. 438.

26. Norton to Delano, Nov. 24, 1921, p. 23.

27. *Ibid.*, p. 26.

28. Glenn *et al.*, *Russell Sage Foundation*, p. 441.

29. *Ibid.*, p. 691.

30. Biographical data from *Who's Who in America*, various editions.

31. Memorandum by F. A. Delano, Oct. 1, 1923, p. 4.

32. "Within a couple of decades [after the initial 'City Beautiful' emphasis in planning], technical and civic leaderships in this field developed to the point where city planning was made an official activity, although not integrated completely into the governmental structure. . . . Planning was considered too sensitive a function to be entrusted to politicians so planning responsibility, and sometimes power, were vested in an independent commission. The members were given overlapping terms that were longer than the terms of the mayors who appointed them. The idea was to take planning out of politics and give it continuity." Joseph M. Heikoff, "Comments," in Harvey S. Perloff, ed., *Planning and the Urban Community* (Pittsburgh, University of Pittsburgh Press, 1961), p. 122.

33. Glenn *et al.*, *Russell Sage Foundation*, p. 445.

34. The survey volumes included: Major Economic Factors in Metropolitan Growth and Arrangement (1928); Chemical, Metal, Wood, Tobacco and Printing Industries (1928); Food, Clothing and Textile Industries, Wholesale Markets and Retail Shopping and Financial Districts (1928); Population, Land Values, and Government (1929); Highway Traffic (1927); Transit and Transportation (1928); Public Recreation (1928); Buildings (1931); Neighborhood and Community Planning (1929); Physical Conditions and Public Services (1929).

35. Quoted in New York *Times*, May 17, 1929.

36. G. L. P., "Regional Plan of New York and Its Environs," *Town Planning Review*, November, 1932, p. 131.

37. John T. Howard, "City Planning as a Social Movement, a Governmental Function, and a Technical Profession," in Perloff, ed., *Planning and the Urban Community*, p. 152.

38. Quoted in New York *Times*, May 28, 1929.

39. *Metropolis 1985: Its Meaning to Business* (New York, RPA, 1961), p. 19.

40. Quoted in New York *Times*, May 28, 1929.

41. Quoted in New York *Times*, May 17, 1929.

42. Glenn *et al.*, *Russell Sage Foundation*, p. 464.

43. In 1931 the board was expanded from 21 to 36 members. In subsequent years, the board has had as many as 42 members.

44. Memorandum to Lawson Purdy, April 1, 1929.

45. Glenn *et al.*, *Russell Sage Foundation*, p. 695.

Chapter II. Commitments

1. The concept of organizational character is discussed in Philip Selznick, *Leadership in Administration* (New York, Harper & Row, 1957), pp. 37–39.

2. Constitution of RPA, Article II.

3. *Minutes*, fifth annual meeting of RPA, May 23, 1934.

4. Staff of the Regional Plan, *The Graphic Regional Plan: Atlas and Description*, Vol. I of *Regional Plan of New York and Its Environs* (New York, Committee on the Regional Plan, 1929), p. 158.

5. *Ibid.*, p. 133.

6. Lewis Mumford, "The Plan of New York," *New Republic*, LXXI (June 22, 1932), 152.

7. *Regional Plan*, I, 133.   8. *Ibid.*, p. 155.

9. *Ibid.*, pp. 165–66.

10. Quoted in John M. Glenn, L. Brandt, and F. Emerson Andrews, *Russell Sage Foundation* (New York, Russell Sage Foundation, 1947), p. 443.

11. Thomas Adams, *The Building of the City*, Vol. II of *Regional Plan of New York and Its Environs* (New York, Committee on the Regional Plan, 1931), p. 36.

12. R. L. Duffus, *Mastering a Metropolis* (New York, Harper & Row, 1930), p. 259.

13. Memorandum from George McAneny to RPA board of directors (prepared some time in 1932).

14. *Ibid.*   15. *Ibid.*   16. *Ibid.*

17. Mumford, *New Republic*, LXXI (June 22, 1932), 152.

18. David B. Truman, *The Governmental Process: Political Interests and Public Opinion* (New York, Knopf, 1951), pp. 139–55, summarizes much of the relevant research.

19. In recent years, RPA has been more successful in recruitment. For example, RPA's New Jersey Committee, set up in 1960 (see Chap. VII), has not experienced a single turndown from any of the sixty-one individuals invited to serve on it or in its subcommittees.

Chapter III. Early Successes and Their Consequences

1. Data on RPA staff are derived from *Annual Reports* of RPA, 1930–34.

2. *Third Annual Report* (1932), p. 5.

3. *Ibid.,* pp. 5–7.

4. RPA *Information Bulletin* No. 9 (Oct. 31, 1932), p. 4.

5. *Third Annual Report* (1932), p. 13.

6. *Second Annual Report* (1931), pp. 10–11.

7. *Fifth Annual Report* (1934), pp. 2–3.

8. These accomplishments are described in detail in *From Plan to Reality,* I (1929–32), (New York, RPA, 1933).

9. Paul Windels, a past president of RPA, speaking in 1961 about the 1929 Plan, stated: "Let me make it clear that these were not all entirely original ideas with the group of pioneers. In addition to their own contributions what this group did was to take many earlier plans and projects and coordinate them into a unified regional concept." From *Metropolis 1985: Its Meaning to Business* (New York, RPA, 1961), p. 20.

10. Arthur Schlesinger, Jr., *The Coming of the New Deal* (Boston, Houghton Mifflin, 1959), p. 284. The Public Works Administration and National Planning Board are treated in *ibid.,* pp. 282–96, 350–53.

11. *Fifth Annual Report* (1934), pp. 5–6, 16.

12. This account of RPA's increasing role in public works projects is based on several *Annual Reports,* particularly the *Seventh Annual Report* (1936), pp. 14–17.

13. *From Plan to Reality,* II (1933–36).

14. *Seventh Annual Report* (1936), pp. 2–3.

15. *From Plan to Reality,* III (1937–40).

16. Wallace S. Sayre and Herbert Kaufman, *Governing New York City: Politics in the Metropolis* (New York, Russell Sage Foundation, 1960), pp. 372–80, describe the powers and duties of the New York City Planning Commission.

17. *Seventh Annual Report* (1936), p. 4.   18. *Ibid.*

19. RPA *Information Bulletin* No. 22.

20. *Fifth Annual Report* (1934), p. 5.

21. Robert C. Wood, *1400 Governments: The Political Economy of the New York Metropolitan Area* (Cambridge, Mass., Harvard University Press, 1961), Chap. 4.

22. These remarks draw on Erwin W. Bard, *The Port of New York Authority* (New York, Columbia University Press, 1943), and on Sayre and Kaufman, *Governing New York City*.

23. Wood, *1400 Governments*, p. 130.

24. Quoted in New York *Times*, Dec. 17, 1931.

25. *Ibid.,* July 2, 1938. Moses' blast at RPA provoked the *Times* to respond editorially on July 9, 1938, defending RPA's good faith and pointing to the recognized distinction of its leaders.

26. These reasons are stated and developed in a resolution adopted by the RPA board of directors on Feb. 16, 1939, recorded in *Minutes* of that date.

27. McAneny reported to the directors of this activity on June 15, 1939. This account is based on *Minutes* of that date.

28. New York *Times,* March 28, 1939.

29. Described in New York *Times,* May 29, 1939, and June 5, 1939.

30. Reported in *Minutes* of RPA board of directors, Sept. 28, 1939.

31. George McAneny, *Reminiscences* (New York, Columbia University Oral History Project, 1949), p. 71.

32. This account is based primarily on *Minutes* of the RPA board for June 15, 1939.

33. *Ibid.*

Chapter IV. The Decline of Purpose

1. *Eighth Annual Report* (1937), p. 2.

2. This account is based on discussions reported in *Minutes* of RPA board of directors and executive committee meetings for 1938–39.

3. *From Plan to Reality,* III (1937–40).

4. Memorandum, undated (written some time in 1941), p. 2, appended to volume of RPA executive committee *Minutes* for 1941–53.

5. *From Plan to Reality,* III (1937–40).

6. See Table 3.

7. This account is based on financial statements and contribution records of RPA for 1940–45.

8. Memorandum from C. McKim Norton to Frederick Horner, noted *supra,* p. 3.

9. Windels served as counsel to the New York State Bridge and Tunnel Commission, 1918–30; associate counsel, Port of New York Authority, 1930–33; corporation counsel, City of New York, 1934–37; chairman, New York City Traffic Commission, 1937; member, Mayor's Business Advisory Committee, 1940–43; counsel, Joint Legislative Committee to Investigate the Public Educational System, 1940–41.

10. Memorandum from Norton to Horner, p. 2.

11. *Ibid.*   12. *Ibid.,* pp. 2–3.

13. *Minutes,* RPA executive committee, May 5, 1942.

14. Staff memorandum to executive committee for consideration at Nov. 12, 1942, meeting p. 2.

15. *Ibid.,* pp. 3–4.

16. Memorandum from executive committee to RPA board, appended to *Minutes* of board meeting of Feb. 4, 1943.

17. *Minutes,* RPA board of directors, Feb. 4, 1943.

18. RPA, *Fifteenth Annual Report* (1944), p. 1. See also *Sixteenth Annual Report* (1945), p. 4, for similar comment.

19. These cooperative arrangements are detailed in RPA's *Thirteenth Annual Report* (1942).

20. Details of this controversy are found in *Minutes* of the RPA executive committee, June 10, 1943, pp. 2–3.

21. See *Seventeenth Annual Report* (1946) and Herbert Kaufman, "Gotham in the Air Age," in Harold Stein, ed., *Public Administration and Policy Development* (New York, Harcourt, Brace & World, 1952), pp. 143–97, especially pp. 179, 184–85, 187.

22. Kaufman, in Stein, ed., *Public Administration,* p. 179.

23. *Ibid.,* pp. 184–85.

24. Staff memorandum to executive committee, appended to *Minutes* of RPA executive committee, Nov. 14, 1945.

25. These figures are taken from RPA, *Memorandum on Program,* Jan. 9, 1949.

26. *Ibid.,* p. 5.

27. Speech by Paul Windels reprinted in *Metropolis 1985: Its Meaning to Business* (New York, RPA, 1961), p. 22.

28. *Minutes,* RPA board of directors, Dec. 20, 1945.

29. Memorandum from RPA staff to board of directors, November, 1949.

30. New York *Herald Tribune,* Dec. 18, 1947.

31. Reprinted in RPA *Information Bulletin* No. 70 (June 1, 1948), p. 6.

32. Speech appended to *Twenty-first Annual Report* (1950).

33. *Ibid.*

34. *Twentieth Annual Report* (1949), p. 2.

35. *Ibid.,* p. v. This group is now affiliated with the Metropolitan Regional Council.

36. The proposal is developed in RPA, *Memorandum on Program,* Jan. 7, 1949.   37. *Ibid.,* p. 21.

38. This and the following data on RPA finances are based on RPA's annual financial statements for 1946–50.

Chapter V. The Rehabilitation of Purpose: I

1. Philip Selznick, *Leadership in Administration* (New York, Harper & Row, 1957), p. 108.

2. David L. Sills, *The Volunteers* (New York, Free Press of Glencoe, 1957).

3. Selznick, *Leadership in Administration,* pp. 109–10.

4. Peter M. Blau and W. Richard Scott, *Formal Organizations: A Comparative Approach* (San Francisco, Chandler, 1962), pp. 228–32.

5. David B. Truman, *The Governmental Process: Political Interests and Public Opinion* (New York, Knopf, 1951), pp. 157–67.

6. Edward C. Banfield, *Political Influence* (New York, Free Press of Glencoe, 1961), pp. 294–301.

7. Blau and Scott, *Formal Organizations,* p. 229.

8. The account of the developments leading up to the proposal for a regional economic survey is based on a memorandum prepared by Fagin for the Rockefeller Brothers Fund, dated May 13, 1955, and interviews with staff members.

9. These meetings are summarized in two memoranda written by Fagin for the RPA files, dated Jan. 21, 1953, and Jan. 26, 1953.

10. RPA, *Metropolitan Region Project,* April 9, 1953, pp. 1–2.

11. This meeting is summarized in a memorandum for RPA files by Henry Fagin, April 7, 1955.

12. The organization and duties of the Project Management Committee were part of the understanding between RPA and the Harvard Graduate School of Public Administration described in a letter of Harold Osborne to Dean Mason, May 19, 1955.

13. Draft report of the Project Management Committee, Dec. 12, 1955, pp. 4–6.

14. *Minutes,* RPA board of directors, Jan. 12, 1956.

15. The study yielded three documents: *The Handling of Metropolitan Problems in Selected Regions* (April, 1958), *The Handling of Metropolitan Problems in the New Jersey–New York–Connecticut Metropolitan Region* (April, 1958), and *Regional Planning Program* (Jan. 6, 1958).

16. *Regional Planning Program,* p. 3.

17. Memorandum, *Proposed Expansion of Program of Regional Plan Association,* Nov. 5, 1957.

18. *Regional Planning Program,* p. 9.

19. *Ibid.,* p. 1.   20. *Ibid.,* p. 13.

21. Dyke Brown, "Ford and Other Foundations in Public Affairs," *Foundation News,* III (July, 1962), 3.

22. *Minutes,* RPA executive committee, March 13, 1958.

23. *Ibid.,* April 8, 1958.

24. *Proposed Program for Regional Plan Association (1958–1961),* p. 4.

25. Memorandum on future program for discussion at meeting of Board of Directors on May 13, 1958, p. 3.

26. *Summary of Major Trends in RPA Program* (from *Minutes* of RPA board of directors, Nov. 12, 1958).

27. Dutchess County officials did not respond initially.

28. *Minutes,* RPA executive committee, Sept. 24, 1958.

29. Other members of the committee were: W. H. Baumer, assistant to the president, Johnson & Johnson, Westfield, N.J.; Amory H. Bradford, vice-president and business manager, New York *Times;* Edwin S. Burdell, president, Cooper Union, New York City; Thomas H. Carroll, vice-president, Ford Foundation; Robert W. Dowling, president, City Investing Company; Luther H. Gulick, president, Institute of Public Administration; H. Bruce Palmer, president, Mutual Benefit Life Insurance Company. Bradford, Burdell, Dowling, Gulick, and Palmer were RPA board members.

30. *The Future of the Metropolitan Regional Council,* report of the Special Committee on Metropolitan Governmental Affairs to RPA, p. 17.

31. *Ibid.,* pp. 1–2.   32. *Ibid.,* p. 17.

33. *Ibid.,* p. 9.   34. *Ibid.,* pp. 7–8.

Chapter VI. The Rehabilitation of Purpose: II

1. Project management committee report to the Rockefeller Brothers Fund, Dec. 22, 1955, p. 5.

2. Report to RPA from the advisory committee of the New York Metropolitan Region Study, Oct. 5, 1959, p. 2.

3. Memorandum to subcommittee on planning, advisory committee of the Metropolitan Region Study, Sept. 8, 1959.

4. Memorandum to advisory committee, Sept. 25, 1959, p. 10.

5. Advisory committee report, Oct. 5, 1959, p. 4.

6. *Ibid.,* p. 11.   7. *Ibid.,* pp. 15–16.

8. *Minutes,* RPA board of directors, Oct. 27, 1959. The following summary of views expressed is based on these minutes.

9. Charles B. Coates & Company, Inc., *Plan of Operation for 1960 and Beyond: Regional Plan Association,* April 15, 1960, p. 8.

10. *Ibid.*   11. *Ibid.,* pp. 15–21.

12. *Ibid.,* p. 12.   13. *Ibid.,* p. 30.

14. Memorandum on RPA program, Feb. 19, 1960, pp. 4–5.

15. *Ibid.,* p. 4.

16. RPA, *Regional Development Program: 1960 and Beyond,* May 4, 1960, pp. 12–15.

17. Notes on conference between RPA and Ford Foundation representatives, April 12, 1960.

18. *Ibid.*

19. *Regional Development Program,* p. 6.

20. *Ibid.,* p. 7.   21. *Ibid.*   22. *Ibid.,* p. 8.

23. *Ibid.*   24. *Ibid.*   25. *Ibid.,* p. 9.

26. *Ibid.,* p. 11.   27. *Ibid.,* p. 12.

Chapter VII. The Implementation of Purpose

1. "Developmental changes are most sharply reflected in personnel turnover. This does not mean just any turnover, such as routine attrition and replacement, but that involving a shift from one type of person to another." Philip Selznick, *Leadership in Administration* (New York, Harper & Row, 1957), pp. 107–08.

2. *Minutes* of RPA board of directors.

3. This account of the New Jersey committee is based largely on a memorandum to the writer from the staff director of the committee.

4. The following account is based on *Spread City* (New York, RPA, 1962). The major findings of *Spread City* are summarized in New York *Times,* Sept. 4, 1962.

5. Memorandum by C. McKim Norton, June 8, 1962.

6. Quoted in RPA news release No. 927, Nov. 15, 1962, p. 1.

7. Memorandum on "Urban Democracy," by John Keith and William Shore, Sept. 6, 1962, pp. 5–6.

8. The plight of the Metropolitan Regional Council is briefly summarized in Robert C. Wood, *1400 Governments: The Political Economy of the New York Metropolitan Region* (Cambridge, Mass., Harvard University Press, 1961), pp. 193–95. Later developments are summarized in a New York *Times* editorial, "The 1500 Little Kingdoms," May 5, 1964.

9. RPA committee on metropolitan transportation, *Proposal for*

a Transportation Commission of the Tri-State Metropolitan Region,
April 10, 1959.

10. Quoted by Walter Binger in a statement for the RPA before
the Subcommittee on Housing of the U.S. Senate Committee on
Banking and Currency, April 26, 1962, p. 4.

11. RPA, *Commuter Transportation: A Study of Passenger Transportation in the New Jersey–New York–Connecticut Metropolitan
Region with Particular Reference to Railroad Commutation,* report
prepared for the Committee on Interstate and Foreign Commerce,
U.S. Senate, 87th Cong., 1st Sess. (1961).

12. Memorandum of C. McKim Norton, June 8, 1962.

13. Statement before Subcommittee on Housing, April 26, 1962,
pp. 7–8.

Chapter VIII. Summary and Conclusions

1. James G. March and Herbert A. Simon, *Organizations* (New
York, Wiley, 1958), pp. 173–77.

Index